BRADLEY BROOK

An American Walks Down an English Stream

If the past makes such a bid for our attention,
the present may escape us.
Charles Dickens

I'm always picking up flints and bits of Roman pottery round the farm.
We English take history for granted.
A Somerset farmer

BRADLEY BROOK

An American Walks Down an English Stream

Dudley Doust

edited by Scyld Berry

photographs by Chris Smith

foreword by Michael Brearley

FAIRFIELD BOOKS

for
my Anglo-American daughters Hannah and Nell,
my Anglo-Anglo-American grandchildren Harry, Lola and Tom,
and, once again, for my English wife, Jane.

Fairfield Books
17 George's Road, Bath BA1 6EY
Tel 01225-335813

First published 2009

ISBN   978 0 9560702 2 7

Printed and bound in Great Britain by
Midway Colour Print, Holt, Wiltshire

Dudley Doust, with Seve Ballesteros

Dudley Doust was born in Syracuse, New York, on 17 January 1930. He was educated at Rochester and Stanford Universities before becoming a journalist for more than half a century. He spent about a dozen years on American newspapers and magazines: firstly, the *Kansas City Star* and then *Time* magazine where, as a staff correspondent, he was stationed in Washington, Atlanta, Chicago, London and – as *Time-Life* bureau chief – in Mexico City. In Britain he was a staff member of *The Sunday Times* and *The Sunday Correspondent.* His work also appeared in other publications worldwide.

Dudley's trans-Atlantic experience, together with the fact that his wife Jane is English, especially qualified him to undertake this book. He lived in Somerset, the setting for it, most of his married life.

Dudley's first six books were about sport: three of them about cricket (two co-authored with Michael Brearley), one about golf, one about horse-racing, and a collection of essays. When he died on 13 January 2008, he left behind several boxes full of papers, containing 15 years and more of indefatigable research – an example being his letter to the Yeovilton museum on the following page – and many drafts of the chapters of *Bradley Brook.*

With the help of Jane, some of Dudley's friends have pooled their resources to publish his seventh book. It was virtually finished: from his papers, it is apparent that the number of areas he still wanted to research had been narrowed down to two. One was the Monmouth Rebellion: he had written to the University of the West Indies seeking help in tracking down the descendants of some deported rebels from West Bradley. The other was a cricket match at Meare which he wanted to research and anatomise in his inimitable way.

Otherwise the book was complete, as the reader will find it. The early chapters were written and re-written many times over. In the several boxes, only one version of the ending was found. It was as if Dudley knew that his journey had reached its conclusion, and he was content.

Scyld Berry, Bristol, February 2009

Westbrook House,
West Bradley,
Glastonbury,
Somerset, BA6 8LS.

Tel: (01458) 850643
Fax: (01458) 850951

February 21, 2001

Fleet Air Arm Museum, Yeovilton
Attention: Research and Records Centre: Fax: 01935 842 630

Dear Sir: I spoke today with Mr. Jerry Shore; he suggested I
fax my query.

I'm a journalist writing a book with the self-explaining title
Bradley Brook: an American Walks Down an English Stream. In it
I talk about incidents that took place alone the route of my
"stream," which comes off Pennard Hill, near Glastonbury, joins
the River Brue below the Tor, crosses the Levels and finally
decants into Bridgwater Bay at Highbridge.

Having said all that, I'm working on a wartime air crash
involving a Hurricane trainer which came down 10.2.43 near East
Pennard. Thanks to help from Sir Desmond Cassidi and your
Graham Mottram, as well as the New Zealand Fleet Air Arm Association, I've tracked down the young New Zealander who was
killed in the accident. Or rather, I've tracked down his name,
his niece and his now-elderly childhood friends. I've seen his
grave at Yeovilton—— all this with a view to painting a word
picture of him in my book.

The pilot, Royce Ivan Cossill, Service Number NZD3268, was
awarded the Defence Medal, War Medal and New Zealand War Service Medal. He was an Acting Leading Airman promoted to Temporary Sub Lieut (A), stationed at RNAS DAEDALUS serving at RNC
GREENWICH with 759 Squadron. His land station was HMS Heron.

Everything so far is fine (I hope so, my research has been on-
going for years) and I'm thankful for all the help Graham
Mottram and others have given me. One piece, however, is
frustratingly missing from the jigsaw. It's this:

I have a photocopy of the pilot's log book, sent me by his
niece in New Zealand. It shows his "first solo" was on Feb 5,
1943 and five days and three flights later he was fatally
injured in the Hurricane crash. In the weeks before his "Pilot
or 1st Pilot" included names which, as a layman, I can only
assume were his flight instructors. These possible instructors
were: F/s Crayford, W/O Winstanley, Sg (?) Jobson Gannaway and,
earlier, F/O Campball and F/O Foster.

With these names and Cossill's data can I hope to reach his
"flight instructors" to round out a picture of the man?

Sincerely,

Dudley Doust

6

Contents

Reproduced by permission of Ordnance Survey on behalf of HMSO.
© Crown copyright 2009. All rights reserved.
Ordnance Survey licence number 100048995.

9

Foreword by Michael Brearley

Dudley Doust was a stocky, tough, indefatigable, humorous man. He looked increasingly wispy as he got older, with tufts of hair spiking up from his eyebrows, or curling from his ears or chest, more and more like his dog Sam.

There were always dogs and horses in the Doust ménage, and, until they grew up and went their own ways, two daughters, Hannah and Nell. One feature of their very English, homely, welcoming but slightly eccentric Somerset house was a list, stuck on the fridge door, of food tried out, and eaten by, the horses. I seem to remember the list included baked beans. The horses, and dogs, were almost part of the family. Dudley was a devoted father and family man.

Dudley had a comfortably ramshackle air about him, but was stronger than one might think. As a childish prank, during the 1978-9 England cricket tour of Australia, a few of us tried to throw him in the swimming pool in Adelaide, but were shrugged off like cubs by a lion.

He had a particular verbal habit, a loud aaagh at what one might have thought was the end of a sentence, but which signified that he would like time to formulate another thought on the subject or to moderate what he had just said.

He had a nose for news, arriving in Lahore the day before riots supporting Benazir Bhutto, being present at the Munich Olympics when the terrorists struck. But he had a nose for more ordinary 'news': he would find the new view, the filled-out picture, the revealing detail.

This is a multi-layered book. As the dedication suggests, with its author's emphasis on Englishness and Americanness, it is a reflection on identity. Dudley was, of course, American. He was also an American who lived for 45 years in England. He even wrote about cricket. But he kept his American passport.

The book is at one level the account of a journey, a walk along a river which, in its form as a brook, ran along the bottom of the field next to the house where Dudley and his English wife Jane lived, and her horses grazed.

But it is far more than this. It is an idiosyncratic social history of the region. Doust links present with past, sees change and identity through time. Close-ups in the present are repeatedly re-scaled as parts of a long-term tapestry. This applies to landscape as much as to people. In Doust's skilful hands, the views we are given zoom in and out. We are (as, he tells us, his surname implies) dust as well as vivified clay. The reverse too happens: what is a mere anecdote from a distant past, like a war-time plane crash, is fleshed out by memory and record, so that we have a tantalising picture of a young man from the other side of the world, suddenly plunging into Pennard Hill and oblivion.

Bradley Brook is a literate, even literary book. We meet on the journey Steinbeck, Hardy, Fielding, Defoe, Gray, Dickens, Eliot (a reference to 'mixing memory and desire'), Tennyson, Malory, Coleridge, and Southey (I could go on). Doust carries what might be a weight lightly. He is ever-curious, insightful, erudite even; but never turgid or out to impress.

In one way or another, we encounter – earthily – an archaeologist, sheep-shearers, a grave-digger, artists, a horse dealer, a feller of cricket-bat willows, a dairy farmer, a colour therapist, an eel fisher, a museum custodian, a vicar, a funeral director, publicans, a fish-and-chip shop owner, and many others. Doust had an American's democratic range of interest and benign attention. He spoke to everyone in the same way, whatever their status.

An event in Pennard, Somerset, links to a Maori settlement – the world is a small place. Doust the investigative journalist ferrets out the story of a young New Zealand pilot whose plane crashed in 1943. He talks to the young man's ex-girlfriends, and his niece. We learn that his forebears included a Maori princess, Pourewa (later Margaret), who married Charles Cossill in the 'first-ever Christian joining of white and Maori partners under European law in New Zealand'. We get a poignant, ramified picture, stretching before and after, of an accidental death during the war.

The book is also a ruminative reflection on what it is to be this particular American living his life in this particular part of rural England. We hear of the Doust family; how his 'oldest-known forebear, fourteen generations ago, was a French iron-worker from Picardy, who came to England near the beginning of the sixteenth century, found work in a Sussex foundry and died in 1568.' Dudley's 'paternal great-grandfather, born in Udimore in 1823 (where the French immigrant was buried), married there in 1855 and straightaway emigrated with his wife to America.' We hear about Dudley's own journey in the opposite direction. He is 'the only member of the family who has returned to live in the Old Country'.

We enter the Doust house in West Bradley, share the views from his bedroom window, the trains of thought, the journeys of the mind as well as of body, we hear of the odd memories stirred there. He refers to his having 'written a good deal about cricket, including three books, but I had never struck a cricket ball in my life … Suddenly, watching a young farmer cut a willow tree, I was lonely for a game I had never played.' But how deeply he entered into this strange custom, how far he went in exploring it!

Dudley's cricket interest started, I think, with his interview with me during a Test match in 1977, which set off our friendship and my respect for him. This first contact became an extended conversation, one that by happy chance lasted a whole extra day when rain washed out play at Lord's, and we had a long lunch, and further lunches, together. I then asked Dudley to write with me my first two books on Test series against Australia, and this is when I watched him at work. The second of these books, *The Ashes Retained,* includes Dudley's chapter on Derek Randall's innings of 150 at Sydney – still, according to the editor of the present book, 'the best reconstruction of an innings ever done; no one got inside the head of a batsman to the same extent.'

And what an evocative image of the émigré – watching the cutting of the willow – that he should yearn to have had a past in the culture that he loves but where he is always an outsider! In the next paragraph he goes back to Syracuse, New York, to his Anglophile household, with *the Illustrated London News* on the coffee table, and the Sunday roast beef and Yorkshire pudding dinners, one of them on the evening of 7 December 1941, the day of the Japanese attack on Pearl Harbour. This was a watershed of identity, for, 'afterwards, America having flexed its muscle, my family seemed to sever its frail links with the home country… After VE day, Americans had an identity of their own.' Identity again, the sameness and the separateness.

Another set of emigrants – Thomas Austin's 24 wild rabbits, from the fields in Baltonsborough near Doust's house – were summoned to Australia, embarking on 6 October, 1859. Settled in Victoria, they colonised Australia 'at the rate of 110 kilometres a year', then 'munched westwards through South Australia, and swept wave upon wave across the Nullabor Plain.'

On the last pages, Doust acknowledges his mixed feelings, but I'll leave that to you, the reader, to discover. Enough to say that this is a book in which the author's exploration of his own identity through change runs like a shadow of the book's external subject.

This is a book that, had he lived, Dudley himself might never have finished. He was stuck, stuck not only in England (as he wrote) but in writer's block. The book was fifteen years in the writing, and when he died in January 2008, he left many versions of each section, up to ten versions of some. All the chapters were there, but Dudley, the perfectionist, the indefatigable researcher, the man overtaken by advancing illness, had lacked the confidence to pull them together and send to the printers.

That we have a book, a coherent whole book, is due to the work of Scyld Berry. Scyld always wanted to see Dudley finish it; now he will take credit only for stringing his pearls together. Like many of his friends, myself included, he admired Dudley as a writer. Indeed many of us learned much from him, from – for example – the high value, as an American journalist, he put on research, from his energy and attention to the telling detail, the story or anecdote or impression that captures a man, a place or a moment.

Like the archaeologist referred to in the book, Dudley dug and dug until the fragments made a picture. So we all longed for him to be confident and decisive enough to complete it. He himself was disappointed not to have done so. But thanks to Scyld these difficulties have been overcome. A labour of love.

I should mention two more people in this introduction. One is photographer Chris Smith, a colleague of Dudley's on the *Sunday Times*, who has made so many journeys himself to the countryside of the book, waiting to find just the right light for a picture. His contribution is vivid and palpable. Chris had for many years travelled all over the world on assignments with Dudley. He says: "I sometimes think that subjects reading about themselves in a Doust interview would learn something about themselves that they previously had not been aware of. When Dudley interviewed people they knew about it – often to their own surprise and enjoyment."

Chris gives a lovely illustration of how engaging and probing Doust was in his work, about an interview in Strasbourg with Ivan Lendl, the multilinguist tennis player. The interview had not been set up in advance but by accident or Dudley's design they stayed in the same hotel as Lendl. After a lot of preparatory work in his own room, Chris said, "Dudley finally said 'C'mon, Smith' – he always used my surname – 'we've got an interview.' So we walked twenty metres down the corridor to see Lendl, who looked decidedly suspicious. We knew he was playing later that afternoon, and Dudley (who was always conscious of leaving time for my pictures) said in his wonderfully direct way, 'Ivan, how long have we got?' 'Till you ask your first stupid question,' came the reply. An intimidating comment in any language. An hour later, Lendl said, 'Dudley, I've got to go, I'm on court in twenty minutes, can you come back later, I'd love to finish our conversation.' That was Dudley, a great friend and companion, and a wonderful colleague."

Finally, Jane Doust, Dudley's wife. Hardly seen in these pages, she hovers in the background, the source and centre of Dudley's life in England, of his home, from where he starts on the journey of the book. Jane is the main pivot that drew Dudley to, and kept him in, England. Jane is as English as Dudley was American, an artist and passionate about horses and riding. She hovers and darts around topics like a butterfly, dipping, settling, flitting, but like her husband evoking individual and perceptive pictures. Both were the children of doctors, and perhaps the eye they both have comes from the particular focus of the clinician. Jane too has been very helpful to Scyld in the preparation of the book that you now hold in your hands.

As Steinbeck (quoted on page 18) wrote: 'There are voices in the ground.' This book is a core-sample of English life, taken from the soil – and water – of Somerset, by this admirable author.

Prologue

My oldest-known forebear, fourteen generations ago, was a French iron-worker from the province of Picardy. He came to England in the sixteenth century, found work in a Sussex foundry and died in 1568. He is buried in a churchyard not far from the Sussex village of Udimore, where his descendants toiled for generations as farm labourers.

My paternal great-grandfather, born in Udimore in 1823, was married there in 1855 and straightaway emigrated with his wife to America. Their voyage in a sailing ship took six weeks and, over the next century and a half, no fewer than four hundred of their direct descendants were born in America. For myself, I travelled from New York to England in the *Queen Elizabeth* in five days in 1961 and, as far as I know, I am the only member of the family who has returned to live in the Old Country.

As we entered the port of Southampton, I stood at the ship's railing – stunned, enthralled by what I saw. There, across the sparkling water, slid a vast fleet of small racing yachts – scores, maybe hundreds of them – their spinnakers blooming in the breeze. This was Cowes Week, the biggest, longest-running regatta in the world.

What a reception! I was in England. From Southampton I travelled up to London on the boat train. I remember leaning forward in my rail carriage, delighting in the names of the stations that swept past the window. *Eastleigh. Winchester. Basingstoke.* The Anglo-Saxon monotony of the words escaped me, I'm sure. In the time between their passage, I'd have looked through my newly bought *Times*. I'd have been looking for stories and *The Times* of London was then the British paper of record, the one we quoted to our editors back home.

The Prime Minister, Mr Macmillan, was reported to be tired and going to stay with the Duke of Devonshire for the start of the shooting season. The main sports story in *The Times* that day was of the England v Australia Test Match in Manchester. Dutifully, I fought my way into a thicket of cricket terms: backward short-leg, stump, and 'bowling into the rough'. Nobody had a first name in the story. In my days at *The Kansas City Star* only prostitutes were stripped of their first names.

A place on the London bureau of *Time* magazine was the assignment I'd coveted. When informed of the appointment I was in Missouri with Bill Mauldin, an anglophile and political cartoonist of the *St Louis Post-Dispatch*. He told me if I went to London, I'd marry an English girl and never return to live in the States. He was right. On my first night I met an English girl who'd be my future wife.

Since then, except for two years in Mexico, I have spent the rest of my life in England. So why am I still unsettled? Why, though my wife, our children and grandchildren are English, have I remained an American citizen? Why, unlike some of my fellow expatriate Americans, have I not sought dual citizenship – instead, being satisfied (and grateful) to have my successive U.S. passports stamped with the words 'Given leave to enter the United Kingdom for an indefinite period'?

It was this search which brought me to the top of Pennard Hill in the countryside of Somerset, my wife's county, where I'm still the outsider. I prefer it that way. My American roots are too old and deep but, from time to time and with increasing intensity, I find myself making up memories of an English childhood.

Pennard Hill

Pennard Hill lies in the English county of Somerset and from its high point, a windmill on Hill Farm, you can gaze westward to the sea. The eye travels for a mile across hill pastures, pleated with hedges, dotted with cattle and sheep, before falling away to present a panoramic view of the countryside. The scene, apart from a distant field of yellow and alien rape seed, is as pale and delicate as an English watercolour. It once moved the poet Thomas Hardy to verse. 'Beneath us figured Tor and lea,' he wrote from an inn on a nearby hill. 'From Mendip to the western sea, I doubt if finer sight there be, in all this royal realm.'*

* The poem, *A Trampwoman's Tragedy*, Hardy's favourite narrative poem, first appeared in *The North American Review* in 1903, and in his collection, *Time's Laughing-stocks*, published in 1909. The ballad, based on an early 19th century incident, tells of the trampwoman teasing her beloved "fancy-man", the horse thief Blue Jimmy, over advances she encourages from their travelling companion, John. In a jealous rage Blue Jimmy stabs to death the hapless John and subsequently is hanged. The murder takes place at the 'Marshal's Elm' inn, which was still an inn when Hardy visited it many years later. The inn now is a farmhouse with bed-and-breakfast facilities; when I knocked, the farmer's wife vaguely knew of the poet's visit but was shocked when I told her of the murder that occurred in her sitting-room.

Incidentally, when Hardy beheld this Somerset scene from near the inn, he was rising 60 years old and on a 150-mile round-trip bicycle journey from Dorchester through what he called 'North Wessex'. What of his bike, or his 'Byke', as he called it? Ah, such is the appetite for Hardy lore that in its August/September 1999 issue the British magazine *Cycle Touring and Campaigning* reported that shortly before his journey the poet paid £20 (now £114.14) for a 'Rover Cob', with its state-of-the-art 'plunger brake, pneumatic tyres and protective chaincase which may possibly have contained a sump to provide continuous lubrication. It also had a bell....'

The fine sight has changed little since Hardy stopped there at the end of the nineteenth century. His 'Tor' is Glastonbury Tor, rising like some gigantic sea creature from his 'lea', that great reclaimed swamp known as the Somerset Levels or, more fancifully, the Vale of Avalon. His 'western sea' is the Bristol Channel which flows south and west and out of picture into the Irish Sea and the Atlantic Ocean.

The scene, often wet and cloaked in mist, is framed and enclosed by west-running hills, the Mendips to the north and the Poldens to the south. And finally, as though to complete a formal, Royal Academy composition, a river carries your eye diagonally, foreground to background, across the picture to the sea.*

* When Henry Fielding, writing in the middle of the eighteenth century, made use of this same scene in *Tom Jones*, he gave it a romantic spin. Into the Levels he plunked a long-gone lake from which 'issued a river, that for several miles was seen to meander through an amazing variety of meadows and woods, till it emptied itself into the sea....' For his fictional purposes, moreover, Fielding enlarged the low Mendip Hills into 'wild mountains, the tops of which were above the clouds.'

In fact, on a rare clear day when the air has been rinsed by rain, and when the tide is in, you could climb the windmill on Pennard Hill and make out the coastline, eighteen crow-fly miles away. It appears as a band of grey, not far from where Daniel Defoe wrote of the Great Storm of 1703 throwing waves 'with furious haste' across the countryside.

The picture seems compact and orderly, altogether English. Quintessentially English: under-stated, quiet, self-contained, content to keep its thoughts to itself. Then, slowly, a secret of the landscape begins to emerge from the mist. Look again at the river. Something is odd about it: it travels string-straight, except for a single right-angle jig, during its passage from Glastonbury to the village of Meare and then, in small twitches, continues westward. It's not natural. It's man-made. And the longer you look at the river and the surrounding landscape, the more you sense – if not absorb – the idea that a lot has gone on out there over the past many centuries.

Originally, there was no river, just a shapeless ooze, a marshland studded by 'lake villages', half-floating on beds of timber and brush wood. These villages were linked by a raised timber trackway which, some archaeologists say, is the oldest known road in Europe. And before that, as one Victorian historian surmised, the drenched landscape presented either 'a gloomy waste of waters, or still more hideous, an expanse of reeds and other aquatic plants, impassable by human foot, and involved in an atmosphere pregnant with pestilence and death.'

Now, 6,000 years later, my eyes wander over the scene. Out on the coast, not far from where the river enters the sea, a pair of tiny grey cubes can be picked out against the skyline: the nuclear power station at Hinkley Point.

Moments later, and nearer, a RAF Tornado, on a training run from Yeovilton Air Station, scorches low over the countryside. The warplane disappears over the Polden Hills, its rumble dissolving into the age-old battlefield of Sedgemoor.

Then, at its own leisurely pace, the landscape reclaims its silence; it now seems haunted, exhausted. The American writer John Steinbeck sensed the same eerie busyness in this landscape. 'It's more than meadows and hedges,' he wrote home from Somerset in the summer of 1959. 'Much more than that. There are voices in the ground.'

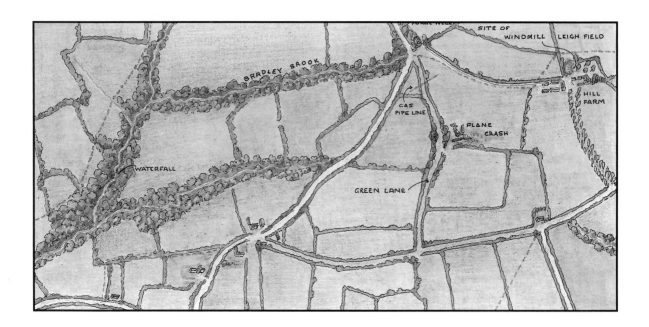

How differently we Americans perceive our landscape. Guided by generations of *National Geographic* picture editors, we determinedly choose to see it as uninhabited, virginal, still-to-be-written-upon and, above all, big, bigger, biggest. Imagine the Grand Canyon: a mile deep and a dozen miles wide, awesome in its shades of reds and browns and blues which deepen with the onset of evening; or our Sequoia trees. Even the monotonous stretches of our Great Plains present their own empty grandeur. "The only thing very noticeable about Nebraska was that it was still, all day long, Nebraska," a Willa Cather character recalls of a train journey taken across the young state in his youth.

These thoughts brought to mind my first assignment as a journalist in England, in the summer of 1961. I'd been in the country only a few days when I was sent from London to interview the abstract landscape painter Peter Lanyon in St Ives, an artists' colony on the western tip of Cornwall. It was evening. We were standing on a quay overlooking the Atlantic when I asked Lanyon why his paintings were so physically small.

A bemused smile crossed his face, as though he himself had considered the question in the past. "Even if my canvasses were bigger than Jackson Pollock's, my pictures would be smaller," he said. "We in England needn't paint big. We haven't got the great land mass behind us." He paused, and went on to explain. "Pollock, standing on the eastern end of Long Island, had 3,000 miles behind him. I've only got 300."

Lanyon's words long have played in my mind and now, some forty years on, I was setting out to apply them in an attempt to paint my own picture of England. After all, if the mighty Mississippi could tell a tale of America, why couldn't Bradley Brook speak for England?

The water's course, from hill to coastal mud-flats, runs only 23 miles, but my journey would cover that distance many times over. Armed with maps, notepads, binoculars, a pocket tape-recorder and such vital source material as human memory, local and national newspapers and Sir Nikolaus Pevsner's invaluable work, *The Buildings of England*, it was my intention to keep the stream and river in mind, if not always in sight, as I wandered through the towns, villages and countryside that lie along its way. I would follow the stories which sometimes led me to faraway places, such as New Zealand, Melbourne, and a hard-scrabble farm community just north of Naples.

I'd start my journey at the stream's source, the pond beneath my feet.

Hill Farm

I had been living for years in a Somerset hamlet in the shadow of Pennard Hill and occasionally I wandered over its fields and up and down its lanes and coombes. To say I was 'looking for something' – other than a good place to walk a dog – would suggest that I was seeking some artificial device to drive along my story. But I think the idea of writing about the hill, the farm pond and eventually the stream began, or at least gathered force, with the haunting story of a Bronze Age man and a piece of flint that was found on the hill.

Some years ago, when the British Gas Corporation was laying a pipeline across Somerset, I went up Green Lane to watch its earth-digger take delicate bites out of Pennard Hill. The machine was manned by a Frenchman, world-travelled in such finely tuned work, and the operation monitored by a British archaeologist. It was the archaeologist's job, indeed his duty to the nation's Department of Monuments, to collect and catalogue the artefacts found along the 40-mile trench.

That morning, 'small find 23', a jet-black, inch-long flint scraper, was unearthed from beside the lane. The archaeologist shook it from its plastic packet into the palm of my hand. I hefted it. It felt heavy for its size which, perhaps curiously, seemed to confirm its legitimacy. What's more, the splinters of light, snapping out of its depths, suggested the flint was furious at being disturbed after all these centuries. "It's from the Neolithic/Bronze Age," said the archaeologist. "Say 3,000-4,000 years old. It's the oldest thing we've found on the hill."

The flint scraper was a "stray", he went on. "You don't find flint in this area. Someone, possibly an outsider wandering along the lane, dropped it and it got scattered into the field." I asked: what was this 'outsider' doing on the hill? The archaeologist shrugged. "Maybe he was on his way down to the Levels. Maybe he was lost. Maybe somebody – or some thing – was after him."

The image of a Bronze Age man, fleeing in fear, returned to mind as I walked up the lane a few days later. I was on my way to an appointment with Adrian Pearse who, with his father, farmed the 150 acres of Hill Farm. Adrian had granted me permission to climb his windmill, which I had done the previous day, and now he would give me a tour of the farm.

When we met in the farmhouse porch – under a stone reading '1884', which seemed oddly 'new' for an English farmhouse – I mentioned the pipeline. I mentioned the archaeologist: an interesting man, I thought. I mentioned the flint scraper. Adrian nodded and bent to tug on his gumboots. I asked him what he made of a Bronze Age man being chased down Green Lane. Adrian straightened up, and nodded again. Yes, he'd seen the trench being dug. He'd met the archaeologist. But, overall, what he had seen and heard only confirmed what he already knew. With that, it seemed plain, the archaeologist was dismissed.

We set out across the cobblestone cattle yard, Adrian leading the way. A tall, bony, 40-year-old bachelor in steel-rimmed glasses, he was dressed in the manner of a conventional English farmer: black gumboots – no fashionable Princess-Anne-green-gummies for him – an old pair of corduroy trousers, a checked shirt, threadbare at the collar, and an oil-cloth jacket, snagged here and there by barbed wire. Less conventionally, he wore a baseball cap, promoting a local farm co-operative. Most unconventionally, the cap was tugged far off to one side, which made him look goofy.

Adrian isn't goofy. He read History at Oxford and like many educated, rural Englishmen he's at ease with a past that lies buried around him. "We English take history for granted," he'd say to me in a later conversation. "We don't marvel at what we've got because it's so familiar. I haven't been abroad much. But I've been over much of England and whenever I go somewhere new, notice bits and pieces of the past in other parishes, I realize I've got them at home. I only have to look."

Our 'look' began at the farm pond. On my Ordnance Survey map, the pond is too small to be realistically rendered. Instead it's represented by a symbol: a clear, bent tear-drop which, in its case, appears poised to drip down and engulf Adrian's much smaller farmhouse. Art, in the case of cartographers, doesn't precisely follow nature: for, in truth, the pond looks small and harmless. It's mucky and irregular in shape. It's shored up by a crumbling wall, and clogged with weeds and bulrushes. As I stood there, trying to form an opinion of my 'headwater', a chill breeze sent a shiver across its dark surface and shuffled through the bulrushes.

Bulrushes. The word stirred up another word in the background of my memory. Cats' tails. A long time ago, in Upstate New York, we called them 'cats' tails'. We'd rub their brown spikes into fluff, then lay the fluff out to dry in the sun. Roll it, smoke it in a sheet of *The Syracuse Post-Standard*. The unformed memory was drifting through my mind, just out of reach, when Adrian's voice broke in. "Titicaca," he was saying. "When we were children the pond was rather like Lake Titicaca. It was a great mass of bulrushes. We'd knock them down and make pathways and platforms, sort of floating islands. We'd go amongst them and disappear."

Then, with something like a chuckle, he suddenly put aside his childish thoughts. "This pond may not look like much," he said, his voice regaining its authority. "But it's a superior pond, the best on the farm. It has been for centuries. Because, you see, it never dries up."

He went on to explain that the pond was one of the oldest features on Pennard Hill. According to the Saxon Charters of Somerset of 681 A.D. – his voice dwelled on the date – the Anglo-Saxon version of the word 'Pennard' was 'Pen-geard', meaning 'Yard of the Cattle Pen'. This suggested, indeed it supported, the fact that there was a settlement up here at least as long ago as the seventh century. "And the settlement would have had animals, you see, and the animals had to drink. So either the pond was built, or a wet spot expanded."

He now was in full pedagogical flow. The cattle no longer drank from the pond. They hadn't done so since main line water was laid up the hill in the early 1970s. Which meant the pond was now obsolete after – what? – twelve-thirteen centuries of use. "Sad," he concluded. "But now we only keep the pond in case of another fire." When was the last fire? "In 1884," he replied. "It burnt the place down. I don't know a lot about that earlier farmhouse but, according to local lore, the fire was caused by cheese running over," Adrian later would tell me. There was something, he added, about an old lady, who had been a child on the farm, being led through wet grass away from the fire.

We reached a second, smaller pond. It was an abandoned Saxon quarry, Adrian said, kneeling to pick up a loose stone. In the twelfth century the quarry supplied limestone in the construction of Glastonbury Abbey. "Inferior blue lias," he said, tossing aside the stone. "You'll find it's used as rubble in the middle of the abbey walls." We moved on.

Turning up his collar against the breeze, Adrian led on to Leigh Field, eight acres of open pasture. "It wouldn't have been as cold as this in Saxon times," he said. "We'd have had cover. The settlement would have been carved out of a dense forest of alder, oak and elm."

'Leigh', meaning 'meadow', was a still-used place-name that first appears in the Pennard charter of 816. There, in a stark, still un-budded apple orchard, Adrian pointed out several ripples in the land that didn't immediately spring to sight: fairly uniform undulations, they ran in parallel down the length of the orchard. "These are the remains of medieval paddocks, hacked out of the wilderness," he said. "When the snow's on the ground and it's beginning to melt, the paddocks are picked out brilliantly. Then, three days later, they're gone."

On January 17, 1930, I was born in Syracuse, an American city a long way north of New York City but not far from the Canadian border. It snowed heavily that day. I *know* it snowed heavily that day because years later I went to the local library and looked up an issue of the local *Syracuse Post-Standard* to see what had happened on the day of my birth. The weather report, printed the following day, said that in the past twenty-four hours two feet of snow had fallen on the city.

Maybe, somehow, my first opening of my eyes to such weather has made me always aware, deep-down, of snow. I can remember, for example, more than once skiing over a hill to school as a boy. I can remember looking out of my bedroom window and seeing no cars parked in the street. There had been cars there the night before – of that I was certain. But now, as if by magic, there were none at all. I slowly realised they indeed were there, but covered by a blanket of drifting snow.

The love of snow plainly was not in my bones. My great-grandfather had come from England where, as far as I could gather, it rarely snowed. William Doust was his name. Doust? What, I wondered, did that name mean? Where did it come from? It came from the French words 'd'Aout', meaning 'of August', said my grandmother, who knew lots about everything.

The definition suited me fine. I took it to mean 'men of August', which didn't make a lot of sense but it had a swaggering, tough-guy ring to it. After all, our 'men of August', I was happy to know, had left England in great numbers in the past century and now were scattered across Australia, New Zealand, South Africa – and heaven knows where else.

Years later, poking through a book of family names (again in the local library), I discovered the truth. The word 'Doust' actually meant 'dust', because far back in Yorkshire history my family might have milled flour for a living and therefore had been covered in flour-dust. When I learnt this, I remember thinking: "'Dust'. That's not as nice as 'Men of August'."

In the same Leigh field, not far from the sunken Pilgrim's Way, was a saucer-shaped dip. It was a bomb crater, said Adrian, grown over, healed and hardly discernible. Would his father know more about it? No, he hadn't yet moved from Shepton Mallet by time the bomb fell. "But he knows about the plane that crashed in Green Lane during the war."

The Central Somerset Gazette, the weekly newspaper serving Pennard Hill, reported on its front page on February 12, 1943, that a local publican was fined £2 for permitting 'a light to be visible' from his pub window 'during the blackout period'. The paper carried a pastry recipe issued by the Government's Ministry of Food, in which potatoes were substituted for flour, a commodity largely imported from Canada during the war. 'Bread costs ships. Eat home-grown potatoes instead,' implored an accompanying slogan. Elsewhere in the paper, the secretary of Somerset's War Agricultural Executive Committee cited 'the shortage of rubber' in warning agricultural workers not to wear 'rubber boots at times when this class of footwear is not necessary.'

Another story announced the formation of a local Goats Club 'to help and advise all interested in this branch of home food production.' Other items, such as a successful scrap metal drive in Glastonbury, likewise were aimed at supporting the war effort. And yet, in accordance with wartime censorship, the *Gazette* ran nothing whatever on the big news that swept word-of-mouth across the hill that week. At about noon on February 10, two days before the paper appeared, an RAF Hawker Hurricane trainer crashed into a field on Hill Farm.

We found Lionel Pearse, Adrian's 60-something father, in the back kitchen of the farmhouse. He was hunched over a wooden table, his eyes closed in concentration and a pair of ham-radio earphones clamped round his head. A mug of tea, glazed in cold milk, rested on the table. When we interrupted him he held up his hand in a shhhh-wait gesture and after a moment more of chit-chat he signed off, 'Ranger II' his code-name. Pulling off his earphones, he said, "Sorry, I've just been reminiscing with a friend in Weston-super-Mare."

Lionel Pearse, like his son, plainly was a man who kept up with the past and, at my request, he re-tuned his memory to the time of the plane crash.

"I didn't actually see the plane crash," he began. "It happened mid-week and I wasn't on the farm." During the war, he explained, he had been a weekly boarder at Sexey's school, some eight miles away in the town of Bruton, and on Friday afternoons he came home for the weekends. "My mother probably would have fetched me that Friday, she often did, and likely as not, she wouldn't have mentioned the plane crash."

They would have travelled back to the farm in the family's Austin 16, a brown, 1928, canvas-topped touring car. In those days the war left its mark on everything, Lionel recalled, even on family motorcars and, according to regulations, its headlights were hooded to shield their beams from enemy aircraft. That Austin was a classic but, he remembered, he'd been embarrassed by it: it was old, you see, fifteen years old, and his school mates poked fun at it.

I wondered: what might have occupied his mind that day in the car? "Likely as not, I'd have been thinking about my ferrets," he said after a moment. "Every Saturday, when I was at home, I'd take the ferrets rabbiting. I'd put a net – we called it a 'purse net' – over a rabbit hole in a hedge. I'd put a ferret down the hole and step back and pretty soon a rabbit would pop out and get tangled in the net. I'd grab him by the hind legs and dispatch him with a chop behind the ears. Rabbits, if in good condition, could make two shillings each in the shops. And if you got half a dozen in a day, that was good pocket money."*

* Indeed, it was very 'good pocket money' for a 12-year-old farm boy; at this time of writing, some 56 years later, 'two shillings' is worth £2.30 or, in total, £13.80 for the half-dozen rabbits; that's $3.68 a rabbit in US currency, $22.08 for the six. A farm labourer only got three or four pounds a week.

In rural areas, the rabbit not only was popular as meat during the war, but its pelt was suitable for crafting a crude pair of gloves. In fact, public interest in the common rodent was so great that local newspapers carried regular 'Rabbit Notes'. One such note I later found was dated February 5, 1943, the week before the plane crash. Under the headline, 'To Bleed or Not', it counselled against cutting the animal's throat directly after killing it: 'this is unwise if you have a good fur rabbit as the blood stains cannot be removed from the rabbit.' Instead, the paper suggested, 'Kill the rabbit. When dead and still warm, hang it up by the hind legs and skin it. Immediately after skinning and before the blood is set, cut the throat. It will then drain and solve the difficulty.'

Lionel Pearse wasn't into rabbit-skin gloves nor, as it turned out, rabbiting at all that particular weekend. Instead, it was the plane crash which would occupy his mind. He heard about it the moment he and his mother pulled into the farmyard, and he hurried to the scene, ignoring his tea. The pilot, who had been helped away from the Hurricane by Lionel's father and a farm-hand, had suffered hideous burns – his leather flying boots were ablaze – and now he was fighting for his life in hospital.

"The pilot managed to crawl out of the cockpit and about fifty or one hundred yards down the field but he was drenched in petrol," said Pearse. "His leather boots were afire, and all his clothes. My father ran across the field and managed to carry him to Jim's cottage over at Forge Well and they got the doctor. They gave him morphine but he died that evening at the hospital in Shepton. He was from New Zealand, I think, or Australia."

Lionel had made his way through the darkness to Green Lane. When the pilot had swept in for a forced landing, the trees had ripped off the undercarriage and the plane had ploughed through a hedge, finishing upside down and in flames. Lionel saw a sheared elm, a smashed hedge and a deep rut slewing across the pasture. A faint whiff of fuel flavoured the air, and the black smell of burnt grass. In the darkness he found no bits of wreckage. Members of the Home Guard, old men he knew from East Pennard, guarded the plane.

Likely as not, Lionel continued, he probably slept badly that night. He certainly would have been excited by the plane crash as well as the normal night view. To the south, on Wraxall Hill, a red decoy light flashed on and off through the darkness. It was, he (correctly) understood, one of a beguiling series of lights that simulated a stretch of coast-line one night, then perhaps a phony airstrip the next. This scheme, devised by the Bomber Command at Shepperton film studios near London, was meant to confuse German aircraft on their bombing runs to and from Bristol and Cardiff. "We understood the flashing signals were in code," Lionel recalled, "so as not confuse the navigators in our own aircraft."

What was more, there was a searchlight battery tucked under Lambert's Hill, off towards Shepton Mallet, and another near his school at Bruton. "From my bedroom window on the farm, I could watch the shafts of searchlights jerking across the sky. They'd probe round, and suddenly they'd cross and centre on one spot. I've seen planes in the searchlights. They were quite pretty to watch."

"I remember the night the Germans bombed Bath," he said. "Lying in bed, I could see the glow of the fires in the sky over the Mendip Hills." Did he see enemy aircraft shot down? "I can't remember," he replied slowly, with a look of apology. "I was used to watching our fighter planes doing acrobatics but, no, I don't think I ever saw a plane shot down."

"The next morning," Lionel went on, "I went down and scrounged round for souvenirs. We picked up a lot of ammunition and I got a lovely chrome landing light. It didn't have a mark on it, and it threw a beautiful beam. I got some switches, too, and a tail light." Where were they now? He shrugged. "I used to keep them up in my room, but I think they're gone."

I wondered: did anyone actually see the RAF plane come down in Green Lane? "Jim Hoare did," Lionel replied, "and he's still around. Likely as not, he'll be down in his cottage at Forge Well."

Should I phone first?

Lionel chuckled. "No," he said. "Jim's geese will let him know when someone's coming."

As I took leave of him, I couldn't help asking Lionel what he was 'reminiscing' about with his ham-radio friend in Weston-super-Mare. "Oh, birds' eggs. Our collections of birds' eggs," he said and, chuckling, returned to his radio set.

For Lionel Pearse, known as 'Ranger II' to his ham friends, there was a whole world out there in the West of England: 'Acorn' in the South Dorset Downs, for example. Or 'Hawkeye', who might be at home in the high, lonely hills of Dartmoor. He'd try 'Acorn', whose code-name was elaborately constructed from the fact that he was a retired army colonel. Acorn's sign-off was backed by the sound of wolf-calls, "a-woo-woo, a-woo-woo-woo", as Lionel imitated it, as though 'Acorn' was pleased to have captured the sound of Britain's primeval past.

I followed a footpath to Jim Hoare's cottage along a high and treeless stretch of farm field, with my stream, just a thread of water, on my right. A breeze blew across the hill, carrying a whiff of wild garlic, and for the first time in hours I felt free of the clutter of history.

Jim Hoare's cottage was only a few hundred yards along the stream. I paused now and then to listen for the reassuring sound of the water trickling through the underbrush. As I approached his cottage, the stream fell silent, or at least was overwhelmed by the clatter of the geese, letting him know someone was coming. When I reached the door, Jim was there, smiling, waiting. One Pennard Hill story-teller had passed me on to the next.

"Your geese, Mr Hoare. What do you keep them for? Watchdogs?"

"No, we eat them," said Mr Hoare, a raw-handed old-timer. "Come in. How can I help?" I told him my mission and he said yes, he had seen the crash. He'd been 29 at the time, and exempt from military service as a farm labourer.

That day he was working this side of the coombe. "I was cutting a hedge back," he recalled, standing at his cottage window, pointing down to a thickly wooded ravine only a stone's throw away. "I heard a plane engine cut out, but I didn't take any notice. During the war we were used to training flights up here on the hill. But when the engine didn't cut back in, I looked up. It was an overcast day. The plane was coming in low over Green Lane and, I'll always remember, his wings were rocking. Next thing, he hit the trees. Then he sort of flipped over into the field and burst into flames."

Jim got to the burning plane about the same time as Lionel Pearse's father. "The pilot crawled out, his boots all ablaze," Jim went on. "Bullets were going off and he tried to shout us away. 'Live ammunition! Live ammunition!' We dragged him clear. We wrapped him in our jackets and got him down here to the cottage. But he was badly burnt and they took him away. He died in hospital."

Jim reckoned the pilot was from "Canada, or Australia, or perhaps New Zealand." With the name Castle. Then Jim said something extraordinary: "I think bits of the plane are still up in Green Lane. In a ditch." Jim and I went up and, with a bailing hook, grubbed up a piece of the plane. It was a twisted bit of aluminium, about a foot long. "That's it," he said. The rivets had rusted and fallen away but enough was there for the curator of the Fleet Air Arm museum at Yeovilton. He identified the scrap of metal as a bit of fuselage from a Hawker Hurricane.

War records revealed that Temporary Sub-Lieutenant Royce Ivan Cossill, 21, son of Andrew Cossill and Euphemia Cossill (née McGill) of Pipiwai, New Zealand, died on February 10, 1943 at the Royal Navy Auxiliary hospital, Sherborne, Dorset. The hospital, a cottage hospital about twenty miles from Pennard Hill, shut down many years ago. Gone are the medical records. However, I learned the hospital had a burns unit, and a nurse who worked there during the war told me she recalls a young New Zealand air pilot who died there of burns.

Cossill was my man.

New Zealand pilot

It was not so much the name Cossill, however, as the place name "'Pipiwai' which caught my imagination. Pipiwai appears in neither *The Times World Atlas* nor New Zealand travel guides and yet, in my mind's eye, I pictured a clearing at some far corner of the British Empire – a Maori settlement, perhaps, with grass huts and carved wooden totems, a place laced with streams and with sheep on a hill. In a scatter-shot search for Pipiwai – and for Cossill – I fired off letters, faxes and phone calls.

In return, a fax came from Pipiwai: 'In 1940 Pipiwai had a population of approx 600, mostly Maori, with just a few white families,' wrote a Maori elder in the settlement. 'It has three sawmills, and a lot of the kauri logs were hauled out by way of bullocks and waterway.' It had a Te Horo school, a Memorial Hall and horses galore, for in those days horses were Pipiwai's main means of transport. It lay amid rolling countryside, streams and farmland, used mostly for dairy cattle. But it had no Cossills. 'I remember one Cossill family,' concluded the Maori elder. 'They lived at Ruatangata, which is 11 kms closer to Whangarei.' Whangarei, he added, is 140 kms north of Auckland on North Island.

The breakthrough message arrived from Whangarei. 'My wife and I have recently read a letter written by you to a Mr David Allison of the New Zealand Fleet Air Arm Museum,' faxed a Robert Henwood. 'This prompted us to write directly to you. My wife, Glenise Henwood, née Cossill, is the niece of Royce Cossill. Glenise is the only direct descendant currently living in New Zealand. She is in possession of Royce's Log Book.' The message concluded: 'Please don't hesitate to ask us for further help.'

Photocopies of the Log Book, family photos, newspaper cuttings, memories were to come flooding in from the Henwoods and, following my appeal to the local newspaper, from Royce's childhood friends. 'After reading your letter in the *Northern Advocate*,' wrote a lady, aged 80, 'I looked into my tin of old cuttings, getting this one of Royce Cossill. Got it photo-copied so here you are with news of him.'

The press cutting was Cossill's 1943 death notice in the *Advocate*. It was accompanied by a photograph, a headshot, perhaps taken for a high school yearbook. The photo depicts a vital, friendly youngster with a strong neck and thick, wavy (auburn, I heard later) hair. His smile is both shy and composed, his attitude one of pleasant tolerance: the popular high school sports star, impatient with all this picture-taking, and eager to get back to the playing field. Indeed, at Whangarei High School, said the cutting, Cossill was 'prominent in Rugby football, boxing and athletics.'

Glenise Henwood sent along a photo of her uncle Royce with his rugger mates, posed round the dangling carcasses of four pigs in an abattoir.

You're next! they seem to be challenging their fifth, and soon-to-be-thumped opponents. Others recalled a gentler Royce. 'He was charming,' wrote a former girlfriend. 'You could almost believe you were the only one. But there were always plenty more waiting in the background.'

She doesn't recall Royce playing sport. 'A little tennis and table tennis, but mostly dancing. We went to all the dances for miles around. We did waltzes and foxtrots. The Lambeth Walk was into vogue.' She remembered the dance music, too: *In the Mood* and *Good Night, Irene.*

Royce began tootling on the saxophone in those days. He tinkered with 'old cars from the 1920s era,' and, together with Maori boys, fished for eels in the creeks. "Royce and I once shot sixty rabbits in a day," recalled his high school 'best mate', Ralph Martin. "Did we sell them to butchers? No-no. They were vermin and we left them lying in the rough."

Clearly, Royce was a young man of many parts and, after all these years, his friends are agreed: 'Happy' Cossill was someone special while, at the same time, 'just a country boy, like all the others'.

The Cossills were New Zealand people from way back, from way, *way* back.

"Royce spoke about his grandfather Cossill being an old English sea captain, and a Harbour Master at Dargaville, across the island," recalled best mate Martin. There is no record of Royce's grandfather being a harbour master but, indeed, he was a sea captain, plying the coasts of New Zealand, sailing once to the polar regions, twice to America, and serving nine months on an American whaling ship.

No wonder Royce thrilled to romantic thoughts of his grandfather who, according to his obituary, died of 'blood poisoning caused by the slipping of a tomahawk'. Read further into the gob-smacked *Northern Advocate* obit on the demise, at 94, of grand-dad Richard ('Dick') Cossill: 'Bluff, hearty, bearded and bronzed by the suns of many summers, plus a dash of good native blood, Mr Cossill looked a typical sea captain. His appearance did not belie his principal calling for, in schooner and steamer, he had seen many parts of the world.'

Dick's seafaring father, Royce's great-grandfather, moreover, led an even more romantic life. Suffolk-born Charles Cossill, founder of the New Zealand clan, came from England to North Island in the schooner *Darling* in the 1830s. A timber man, a sawyer by trade, he was lured there by the kauri tree, 'the finest timber my eyes have ever seen,' according to Captain James Cook, who first viewed it during his voyage to New Zealand a half-century earlier.

In Captain Cook's time, North Island was covered by an estimated four million acres of the straight-grained kauri trees, much prized for ships' spars and masts. These stands of tree were much denuded by the time Charles Cossill arrived and yet he joined in the massive on-going slice-down of the forests, a project which, in the words of an early New Zealand poet*, left 'a silent, skeleton world; dead and not yet reborn....'

* B.E. Baughan in *A Bush Selection*

In 1836 Charles married a Maori princess, Pourewa – each signing the marriage certificate with an illiterate's 'X' – in a ceremony thought to be the first-ever Christian joining of white and Maori partners under European law in New Zealand. The bride, Pourewa, who became 'Margaret' in the white world, gave birth to Richard, the first of her five children, in 1837; and, in turn, Richard's wife, Sarah, gave birth to Royce's father, Andrew, in 1881. Andrew forewent the family traditions of seaman and sawyer and, instead, tilled the North Island soil which once was covered with forest.

The future airman Royce, youngest of three brothers, was born in 1923 and, on leaving school, joined his father on the family's Ruatangata dairy farm. The youngster, a rare fourth-generation Kiwi, joined the local Young Farmers Club and, according to his aforementioned best mate, "became a Herd Testing officer and a keen learner of stock judging. He had a good eye for confirmation."

By the age of 17, Royce, according to another friend, also had a keen eye for the air; he was bitten by the flying bug while watching single-engine planes "spluttering overhead on their way from Auckland Aero Club to the air races at 90-mile beach" at the far north of the island. "I remember him telling me he was going into the Fleet Air Arm," his girlfriend told me. "He seemed to be excited but I think he felt it could be dangerous. I think you know about everything else."

In September of 1941 Royce left New Zealand on the *Edinburgh Castle*, bound for England, his forebear's homeland – and for war. With him he carried a leather-covered Victorian Bible on which he inscribed his name and '9/41', the date of his departure from home. It is easy to picture the 19-year-old as the troop ship slips out of Auckland harbour under the cover of darkness. He's standing at the rail, gazing at the harbour's great landmark: the extinct volcano on Rangitoto Island, now etched against the night sky.

Standing there, Cossill perhaps gained some obscure comfort from the fact, known to Kiwi schoolchildren, that Rangitoto has not erupted in 800 years. And yet, given the setting, given his frame of mind, Royce's thoughts may well have settled on some awful symmetry. His seaman great-grandfather, an Englishman, had landed here in Auckland, had lived and died in New Zealand. And now, nearly a century later, he himself, an airman, was sailing away from his native New Zealand ... towards what fate in Europe?

Trained first in Britain, Royce was sent to Canada for flying instructions. By then, his best mate Ralph Martin had joined the air forces and at the same time was training elsewhere in Canada. From there both men were sent to air bases in the south of England and, although they corresponded, their paths would never cross again.

By the end of 1942 Cossill was stationed at the Royal Naval Air Station at Yeovilton. There his training progressed from the Tiger Moth, an aircraft used to 'familiarise' fledgling pilots with the English landscape, through the Harvard to the Master II aircrafts. On February 5, 1943 he made his solo flight in a Hawker Hurricane. Five days and three flights later, on February 10, 1943, Cossill took off from Yeovilton in a Hurricane.

On that day there was much air activity over the south of England. The next morning, February 11, *The Times* reported: 'Several places in the south of England were bombed and machine-gunned yesterday afternoon by enemy raiders which attacked from low clouds. Two of the raiders were destroyed.'

At the same time, Royce's pal also was flying in the West of England. "I'd taken off from an airfield near Reading," Ralph Martin recalled. "I was with an instructor in a Tiger Moth. It was a lousy day. Shocking weather. Low clouds. We rarely saw the ground. We got lost and landed at a tiny airstrip in Gloucestershire." Not far away, and in the same foul weather, Royce came out of the low clouds in Somerset and crashed his stricken aircraft on Pennard Hill. In what was to be his last Log Book entry, the crash was noted as an 'accident which was fatal'.

It was only days before Martin knew of his friend's fate. "Royce and I had arranged to meet in London at the NZ Forces Club, when we both had weekend leave," Martin recalled. "It was there I was to learn that he had died after an air crash. I asked a couple of Fleet Air Arm chaps sitting at the bar if they'd seen a fellow called Royce Cossill. They told me they'd been to his funeral the day before."

Cossill's Log Book and his personal belongings, including the leatherbound Bible, were sent to his home in New Zealand and, not long afterwards, his parents received an American flag from a U.S. Senator from New York State. The Senator, wrote the *Northern Advocate*, had met Sub-Lieutenant Cossill 'on a bridge spanning the border between Canada and America.' They became friends and the Senator loaned Royce his car and his speedboat. The Senator was 'deeply affected' by the news of his death.

At Christmas 2001, I received a package from Cossill's niece and her husband. It included the leatherbound Bible with 'Royce I. Cossill, F.A.A. 9/41' inscribed on the fly-sheet. "This is Royce's Bible which was returned with his possessions," Glenise Henwood explained on an accompanying

Christmas card. "We believe Royce is with you and that it's fitting that you should have it."

The following summer Bob and Glenise made a tour of Europe. They stayed with my wife and me in Somerset. We visited the field where Royce Cossill crashed on Pennard Hill. We visited Yeovilton, where his remains are buried in the Royal Navy graveyard behind the fifteenth century St Bartholomew church. As we approached the walled graveyard, we paused to watch an aerial exercise taking place above the air station. A Sea King helicopter lumbered across the blue sky and from it fell a parachutist. As his canopy bloomed safely open, I wondered if he was rehearsing a drop into enemy land, Iraq perhaps? Or was he practising a routine escape from a stricken aircraft?

I glanced at Glenise but her expression gave nothing away and we passed through a wrought-iron gate and into the naval cemetery. It's a tidy little cemetery, with regimented rows of headstones. This pleased Glenise. "It's lovely," she said. "It's so small. I expected to find hundreds and hundreds of graves."

We found her uncle's headstone. Row C, Grave 1. She knelt beside it and, extending her cupped fingers, gently lifted a tiny mauve flower that was growing there. "A wild candytuft," she said and, after a moment of reflection, she stood. She looked up and noticed the green fronds of the palms that border the churchyard. "Look. Look! Those are cabbage trees. They're native to New Zealand. Back home the cabbage trees attract the tui bird. It's a beautiful bird, the tui. Beautiful. And it's blessed with such a strange and beautiful song." She smiled. "Sort of a beckoning call."

Pennard Hill is no more than three miles long, half a mile wide and, according to the richly detailed Ordnance Survey sheet ST 53 NE, never higher than the 125 metres shown by the fine, red contour line curling under the windmill.

Still, the hill enjoys a measure of fame: it appears on William Smith's 1815 Map of England and Wales, known among cartographers as 'the world's first fully-coloured geological map'. Smith, 'the father of British geology', wandered over the hill in 1801, collecting fossils. 'The Land toward the top of this Hill,' Smith wrote in an undated document now residing in the University Museum, Oxford, 'has all that early verdure in the spring and fine sweet herbage which is common to the Land upon the same Substratum in the neighbourhood of Yeovil, Montecute, etc....'

Today, nearly two centuries later, the hill is still vividly green and the pastures, while depleted of many hedgerows, remain scented by wild marjoram and garlic. I am told that Smith, with no windmill to climb, would have been denied my view of the steep, wooded coombe that carries Bradley Brook off the hill and, in the trees below, my glimpse of the notched stone tower of West Bradley church. And the windmill has gone now, dismantled and sold.

Tree-feller

Doug Bush was a tree-feller. "Pennard Hill was my pitch. I worked from my 21st birthday until I joined the army," he told me one evening at the Greyhound Inn in nearby Baltonsborough. "In those days, before the war, you brought your own tools on your bicycle. You hung the three axes over the crossbars, like that and this, with the handles tied in under the seat. Then your saws, three of them, were tied along the top bar. Generally, you had somebody to take your sledge hammer and wedges.

"Then you had your lunch. Generally bread and cheese, with a raw onion, and a bottle of tea – flasks were hardly the thing in those days." He chuckled. "In the dead of winter, we'd build a fire and stand the axes round the fire to get the frost out because, you see, if they were cold when you went to work, pieces of metal could come flying out all over the place.

"In those days, it was all piecework," Bush went on. "Nine shillings for 100 cubic feet of hard wood but if you were felling the soft woods, the firs, that was only seven shillings and sixpence. With the oak and the ash and the elm you had to allow 17% for the bark, which you didn't get paid for. To get your cubic feet, you multiplied your length by your girth twice and divided by 144. We used to say, 'multiply your length by your girth twice and divide by twelve twice'. That made it easier.

"And all the time we'd be looking and listening for rabbits. In the wartime, you see, rabbits were the main meal for country people and up in the coombe there were hundreds of rabbits, rabbits galore. We'd keep our eyes and ears open so's if there was a stoat around, because once a stoat got on to the trail of a rabbit he wouldn't get off, not until he'd mesmerised it and killed it.

"All he'd do is get on the top of the rabbit's back and you'd hear the rabbit screaming."

Doug Bush finished his pint of cider and, excusing himself for the Gents, got to his feet and limped towards the back of the pub. Long ago, he'd injured his right foot, got it trapped under a falling tree in the coombe.

Budgerigars

'As caged birds they are as interesting as can be possibly imagined… constantly billing, cooing, and feeding each other, and assuming every possible variety of graceful position. Their inward warbling song, which cannot be described, is unceasingly poured forth from noon to night, and is even continued throughout the night if they are placed in a room with lights, and where an animated conversation is carried on.'

John Gould, in his Handbook to Birds of Australia (1840-1888)

My last panoramic view across the countryside came in a high field alongside the sheer, wooded bank of the coombe. One day, while absorbed in the view, my concentration was nagged at by a curious and quiet drama unfolding in a field below. Someone in a red tractor was hay-making, circling the field behind the farm labourer Ken Mills' tied cottage. The work was monotonous, despite the radio headphones clamped to his ears, and he later told me his mind had gone wandering.

He had been thinking with frustration about his budgerigars.*

* In Victorian England when, as the English still like to say, 'the sun never set on the British Empire,' the nation's pride in world domination was expressed in London clubs and country houses by the display of stuffed birds and beasts brought back from exotic corners of the Empire. For example, in the 1830s a stuffed budgerigar (or warbling grass parakeet) adorned the rooms of the Linnaean Society in London's Soho Square. That dead bird was the only budgerigar seen in England until 1842 when the Englishman John Gould managed to send back two live ones from New South Wales. An ornithologist, taxidermist and bird artist, Gould was on the remote Namoi Plain gathering material for his seminal work, *The Birds of Australia*. In her biography, *The Ruling Passion of John Gould*, Isabella Tree writes: 'That December the birds thronged near Gould's encampment near Brezi. They were breeding in huge numbers in all the hollows of the tall eucalypti that grew on the banks of the Mokai, and fed in flocks of many hundreds upon the grass seeds on the plains, descending in great noisy crowds on the pools by Gould's tents to drink. In the intense heat of the day most of them fell silent and withdrew into the gum trees, where they disappeared as if by magic among the bright green leaves.' The Aboriginal word 'betcherrygah' means not only the bird itself but 'good eating'. According to the World Budgerigar Organization, Britain has more budgerigar owners than any other country, about 9,000.

The three young ones hadn't got their adult feathers and wouldn't be ready for the upcoming South Hampshire Budgerigar Show. His thoughts then drifted to Candelabra. In times of boredom, such as hay-making, his thoughts always drifted to Candelabra. He wished he had another budgie like her. Best bird he'd ever had. He and his wife Jean had plaques and cups to prove it. Smashing little thing: Cinammon Light Green, with a long, deep mask and a special, aloof look about her. He imagined her perched on his forefinger, her needle-sharp talons digging into his calloused skin. Or perched on his head, lifting his hair, rather like a school nurse looking for nits.

Ken and his wife kept budgerigars, scores of them, in a huge cage on the other side of the cottage. He'd been thinking vaguely of them when he noticed a sparrow-hawk out of the corner of his eye. Only a scrap of black in the sky, the hawk had taken up a position behind the tractor. "I always watch for sparrow-hawks," he explained. "They usually come out of the hollow of the elm tree, over in the hedge. They follow me, keeping me company. Fantastic birds. Wonderful the way they spot a mouse or a mole or a rabbit chopped up in the cut grass, then drop out of the sky to get it."

That day, however, the sparrow-hawk wasn't so fantastic. In fact, it was hopeless. It hovered expertly enough, wings trembling in the currents of air, looking like a tiny para-glider being pulled by an invisible cable attached to the tractor. But, once it spotted its fresh carrion, its plummet was all wrong – even I could see that from the hill. Half-way down, the bird would check its speed, sort of collapse, flutter aimlessly and altogether miss his chopped-up prey. Then it would remain on the ground. Twice Ken stopped his tractor and left it throttling as he swung down from the cab.

"He was just a young 'un," Ken later said. "He didn't seem to know what the game was all about." In each case, Ken found the sparrow-hawk undamaged, tenderly eased it up out of the cut grass and the three of them – Ken, the sparrow-hawk and the tractor – would resume circling the field. This went on for some time, perhaps three or four circuits, before the young hawk, bored or frustrated, drifted away. It settled on the peak of Ken's cottage. Such a roof perch, I would learn, meant danger.

On his next circuit, Ken stopped his tractor under the perched bird. He switched off his tractor engine and yanked off his headphones. He dismounted the tractor and, cupping his hands, shouted up at the hawk. He clapped his hands. He flung a stone at the bird. He disappeared into his cottage and returned with his spaniel. He showed the dog the bird. The dog wagged its tail. Ken stood there, looking up. Finally the hawk flew off and returned to the hollow elm in the hedgerow. Ken resumed his mowing.

Ken later explained his – and the bird's – seemingly curious behaviour. "Sparrow-hawks will attack and terrorise cadged budgerigars," he said. "They'll swoop down on to the wire netting that covers the budgie house and wang into it with their talons. Jean and I once found a dead budgie in the cage. Its neck had been broken from crashing round in terror." Ken seethed in anger at the memory. "The bastard. The cruel bugger. A friend of ours went out one day and killed a sparrow-hawk with her bare hands."

I later heard that Ken shot the young sparrow-hawk. He denies it. "I couldn't do that," he said. "The sparrow-hawk is a protected species." He smiled ambiguously, then snapped, unambiguously: "But in my house, so is the budgerigar."

Waterfall

Jim Hoare's cottage is named 'Forge Well'. You'd have thought such a simple place-name meant just what it said: a forge had been round there somewhere, some time in the past, and a well to supply water to cool the glowing red metal. Perhaps a crimson-faced smith had once lived in Jim's cottage. That was the image I'd been carrying in my mind when, leaving Hill Farm, Adrian disabused me of such a chocolate-box notion.

To be sure, there was a well, abandoned and buried in bramble, across the road from the cottage, said Adrian. You could see it; it was on the Ordnance Survey map, marked with a 'W'. But, he insisted, no forge ever existed near Jim's cottage. The word 'forge', you see, was a corruption (and contraction) of the Medieval Latin term *furce judiciales*, meaning 'gallows', Adrian explained. "The Glastonbury monks kept their land records in Medieval Latin. And when they wrote 'furce', they were referring to a gallows that stood elsewhere on the hill – long after the Romans had gone." Adrian had looked. But he'd never found evidence of any gallows.

I crossed the road, parted the underbrush, and started down the coombe. Within moments I was deep in cool and dappling under a canopy of oaks and elms. As I made my way deeper, anxiety passed over my skin. I didn't much like this place. I'm no wimp, or at least I don't think I'm a wimp, but I'd experienced this feeling before and, not for the first time, I thought of Richard Adams, the English nature writer and novelist of *Watership Down* fame.

'The American view of nature differs markedly from the British,' Adams wrote elsewhere. 'The British nature-lover sees the country (even the moors and mountains) as a safe and tranquil retreat…. The American, however, experiences his nature in a vast continent, much of which is still wild and untamed…. Certainly the country is beautiful – in places – but it can also be dangerous and overwhelming, or dull and uncomfortable.'

I continued down the coombe, kicking through the underbrush, glancing for a 'waterfall' on my Ordnance Survey map. There was also a stone I wanted to see, which was said to loom over the path, not far above the waterfall, on which generations of hill people have carved their initials. The farmer Graham Golledge told me: "The stone was sacred. It was secret. We didn't want people to find it." Graham, in his fifties, is a romantic character, with a face full of hair; and, as a boy, the stone had touched his imagination. "We used to hide a meat skewer in a crack in the stone. We used it to scratch secret messages."

From somewhere a woodpecker beat out a tattoo. I listened. He fell silent. I held still. He began again. I looked for him up through the dense cover of ferns. Then I saw the stone, a great slab of sandstone, tons of it, perhaps twenty feet high and as many wide, poised above a honeycomb of badger setts.

I found the waterfall. It's small, but the water falls in beautiful braids. I found some holes under the lip of the falls. "As boys, we'd play games," a young local once told me. "Who dared to stick his arm furthest down the hole?" Then I noticed the initials are cut in orderly, vertical columns. Such discipline speaks of respect for the stone and my urge to add my initials dissolved. To cut them in would be disrespectful, a cheek. It's their stone, not mine. Not for the first time, I'm reminded: I'm an outsider in England. I've chosen to be. I'm not a group-joiner.

This thought, in turn, called to mind a bar in Kansas City, Missouri. The bar was near the *Kansas City Star* building. In the 1950s, we reporters gathered there at the end of the day. The *Star* had a romantic, fastidious, literary tradition – Hemingway once worked there – and we listened with care when an editor joined us. "Always remember," one said, placing his words like a tablet before us, "a good reporter is an observer, not a participant."

I stopped to pull out my survey map. The stream's descent was dot-dashed on the map and by finger-measuring its crooked passage, top to bottom, I roughly estimated its length through the coombe at maybe two-thirds of a mile. Then, finding the map's contour lines, again top to bottom, I reckoned that in this two-thirds of a mile, the water fell about 170 feet, the biggest drop in its course to the sea. Nothing dramatic.

West Bradley

The centrepiece of my hamlet, West Bradley, is the church. Sir Nikolaus Pevsner, the Leipzig-born art historian, dismissed it in his classic study of English buildings as 'Perp and not of importance'. I thought: what cheek! Sir Nikolaus had best not speak that way to West Bradlians.

Our unshowy church, with its crenellated, four-sided tower rising only some fifty feet into the Somerset sky and dating back to the fourteenth century, we find charming beyond measure. How, in my American eyes, can Pevsner be allowed to shrug off a perfectly wrought building that pre-dates Columbus's sighting of the Americas? Besides, West Bradley's church already holds a place in our family history. Our first daughter, Hannah, was married there and I remember bicycling up the following morning to clear confetti from the walk with a dustpan and brush.

In the churchyard, near its wooden gate, I gazed down at the grave of Nancy Ethel Maidment, died 29th October 1987, aged 69 years. A sweet, frail spinster who lived only a few fields away with her bachelor brother, George. Nancy was the most recent of thirty-two Maidments to be buried in the churchyard. We had known and loved Nancy for her cheery smile and wave as she rattled round the roads on an old tractor.

I wandered round the churchyard in search of a 'story'. But none was obvious. There were many examples of 'In Loving Memory', of course, but in accordance with English reserve, I could at first find no deeper show of public emotion than a 'Dear Mother and Gran'.

Churchyard. Since my schooldays, this always has been a picturesque and comforting word – made so, of course, by those lines from Gray's *Elegy Written in a Country Churchyard*. 'The ploughman homeward plods his weary way/ And leaves the world to darkness and to me.' Splendid stuff. And, later on in the poem, 'The short and simple annals of the poor' and 'Far from the madding crowd's ignoble strife', which must have moved Thomas Hardy as profoundly as his hilltop view of the Somerset Levels.

One day I'd probably be buried in a churchyard, not Thomas Gray's model in Stoke Poges, Buckinghamshire, but here in West Bradley, Somerset. The notion brought to mind my forebears' resting place in America and the word 'cemetery', as explained in a folder called *A Walking Guide to Historical Oakwood Cemetery (in) Syracuse New York, est. 1859.*

The folder, while neglecting to point out that secular, multi-cultural America almost certainly would demand a separation of the word "church" from (grave) 'yard', says: 'The word cemetery, used for the new burial grounds, was a good indicator of their founders' intent: derived from the Greek word for sleeping chamber, a rural cemetery was considered a next home, of a sort, where relatives and friends could sleep in peace.'

Oakwood Cemetery is a vast ground, 160 acres containing some 57,000 graves, the cemetery back home where my forebears are buried round the marble acorn that sits like a big Humpty Dumpty in an egg-cup. Burial records for the West Bradley churchyard date back to only 1633, and ultra-conservatively you have to add a couple of hundred more burials there in the previous two centuries, which gives as many as 700 different human remains altogether. That, to me, seemed a surprising lot of remains in a burial ground which once was smaller, and never larger, than half an acre.

"That doesn't surprise me at all," said Ray Loxton, the local grave-digger. "I'm always hitting bones in West Bradley. It's one of the most crowded churchyards in your part of Somerset. I've done about seven or eight to ten graves at West Bradley – they are set west to east, except the vicars who are east to west, so he can look over his flock. I'm digging over old graves all the time. Put the bones in the dirt pile – then push them down round the casket after the family's gone. You always find bones at West Bradley, sometimes a skull, which you'll have to smash up. My worst experience was when I was buying stuff in Wells, when I realised there was a funeral at 10.30 in West Bradley. I hurried back and heard *Lord is my Shepherd* and found the grave had fallen in over by the conker tree…. Got there five minutes before they came out – luckily they were singing four hymns rather than three – and got it cleared."

Beyond the churchyard is Bradley House, with its broad lawn and a fish pond prettily covered in water lilies, which in turn gives on to a low row of crab-apple trees. Pevsner says: 'A remarkable sight and difficult to explain…. Can this plan be an Elizabethan conceit?' It may, in fact, pre-date Elizabeth for the Glastonbury monks are said to have built it, along with huge fish ponds above and below the house. Carp were stocked in a linking, underground channel and until recently – 1988 – a stone block could be lifted in the cellar to gain access to the stream.

The traditional owners, the Allens, were long the dominant farmers and land-owners in West Bradley, along with the Maidments and the Cottons. Of the churchyard's eighty-odd extant graves, a quarter are occupied by those families. There are countless more crumbled-away graves, for the church has been the hub of the community since it was built more than half a millennium ago.

For instance, what happened to the four Laver infants? They rest in two, side-by-side graves. The first to die was 'Frank Peddle, third son of Edwin and Jesse Laver, who passed away on August 7th, 1879, aged 2 years.' He lies in a grave by himself. Beside him, under a larger stone, are the remains of his sister Ruth, 3 years and 4 months, and his brothers Bertram Henry, 4 years and 7 months, and Guy, 1 month. They died, respectively, on February 17th, March 29th and April 4th of 1883. Or, I reckoned in a few moments, within seven weeks of each other.

The longer I studied these brief inscriptions, the more poignant their story became. What took them away? A smallpox epidemic? Diphtheria? House fire? And, after losing little Frank in 1879, what numbing grief must have hit their parents at the deaths of their three other children four years later. First, Ruth dies, then about a fortnight later Guy is born. Twenty-five days later Guy's brother Bertram dies, and six days after that Guy himself passes away.

In light of this quadruple tragedy, you might expect the parents to be buried near their children. I searched up and down the uneven rows of graves but none marked the remains of Edwin or Jesse Laver. Had they started a new life far away? Was their grief too awful to be reminded of through the whole of eternity?

Indeed, two branches of West Bradley Lavers emigrated to Australia in the mid-nineteenth century, each in later generations adding a name to the list of distinguished Australian sportsmen. One was Frank Laver, a cricketer who represented Australia on a tour of England in the early twentieth century. The other was Rod Laver, the world champion tennis player.

As for Edwin and Jesse, there may be a clue to the depths of their sorrow, and perhaps to their disillusionment with God's cruel whimsy. If so, it lies in the Biblical quotation, now eaten into by lichen, that the Lavers chose to have cut into the foot of Ruth's, Bertram's and Guy's gravestone. It reads: 'Not my will, but thine, be done.' These words are from Luke, patron saint of physicians, those medical practitioners who failed to heal the Laver children.

'I went to West Bradley, and had Wm. Clark with me, to number the Ant-Hills in my ground in Baltonsbury (sic) North-Wood, in order to have them cast,' writes Claver Morris in *The Diary of a West Country Physician* in his entry for 2 March 1721.

'I had into the Inclosure Henry Bull, his 2 daughters, & Thomas Pippin, to help me: but we could not quite do it before Night, though we all 7 began about it at 11 o'clock, & told (by sticking Half Sparrs, 1200 of white & 1200 of red, into every Ant-Hill, and partitioning the ground with 2 lines and 60 paces distance each from the other) – 11400. I left the remainder, which were about 500, to be number'd by Henry Bull, the Night preventing the finishing this work.'

I went to Dr Morris's field which borders the stream. It was, I understand, only the fourth in the country to be enclosed under an Act of Parliament. But now it is two fields and a slender strip of land, owned by three different neighbours. What would Morris have done with the land? I don't know, but now it is put over to turnips, feeding grain, and Friesian cattle – and ostriches, for their meat. Times change, farming adapts.

Our house, Westbrook House, is Victorian and from our big bedroom window I can see the row of willow trees lining Bradley Brook, running through our fields. Also I can see the signpost* at the crossroads outside the front gate. A 'rural finger-post' in the language of the highway surveyor, it stands aslant in a hedge of hawthorn, bramble and ash. It is surrounded by cow parsley and overlooked by a willow, whose slender, whippy branches are pollarded every few years.

*Somerset finger-posts differ from those in neighbouring Dorset, which are capped by open circles, often knocked off by vandals, and those in Devon, which wear cast-iron galleons, all sails abloom. "Never trust the miles on a finger-post. They're all a bit off," says a retired Somerset roads surveyor, his voice chipping the adage in stone. He went on to explain that in the old days parish councils were charged by the yard for roads built within their boundaries, and when it came time to pay up, a quarter- or even a half-mile would be lopped off the invoice.

West Bradley's cast-iron finger-post, or a wooden one, has stood at the cross-roads throughout living memory – except during World War II when, like other finger-posts in the nation, it was removed to confound enemy invaders who never invaded. Capped by an ornament in the shape of a four-sided pyramid, it has three fingers. They read:

West Pennard	1¾
Glastonbury	4¼
Shepton Mallet	7¾
Baltonsborough	1¾
Parbrook	1¼
East Pennard	3¾

These images prey on my mind. All those pure-English place names. All those distances measured to the last fraction of a mile. In recent years, however, I've come to realise how these messages reflect profound differences between England and America.

Think first of my native country, and specifically of the word 'Syracuse'. It's a foreign word, chosen by the city's late eighteenth century settlers who came from Sicily to build a canal. I can think of other towns and cities near Syracuse whose names speak of the same romantic, immigrant-longing for the Old World. Ithaca, Geneva, Marcellus and Cicero come readily to mind. Marathon, Frankfurt, Norwich, Liverpool, and even the hilly, bustling little city of Auburn which, owing to somebody's fanciful memory, borrows its name from 'the loveliest village of the plain', *The Deserted Village*, portrayed idyllically by the Anglo-Irish poet Oliver Goldsmith in 1770.

Forebears and place names

'America is always throwing out these old-world hints,' E.M. Forster wrote in his essay collection, *Two Cheers for Democracy*, 'and then withdrawing them in favour of America.'

When I had travelled from the United States to England, I had arrived on the *Queen Elizabeth* at Southampton on August 1, 1961. Conversely, my great-grandfather had sailed from England to the United States, landing in New York in the spring of 1855. We each were to settle and spend the rest of our lives in an adopted country.

William Uriah Doust, aged 21, was married to a Sarah Green in March of 1855 in the Sussex village of Udimore (population then: 440) and, according to the obituary that appeared in the *Syracuse Post-Standard* at his death in 1904, they 'immediately started for America, making the trip across the Atlantic in a sailing vessel.' The trip took six weeks, according to notes written by their first son, my grandfather Isaac Uriah, who was born the following year in Syracuse, New York.

Once in New York, William's and Sarah's onward journey could have been by one of three means: rail, packet boat on the Erie Canal, which linked the Hudson River with Lake Erie, or by the time-honoured stage coach. The words 'stage coach' now may have a romantic ring, but the facts were something else. 'With the perfume of tar-grease and four reeking horses,' wrote one contemporary traveller, 'the liability to sea-sickness of the passengers by reason of rocking and rolling over corduroy roads, and the crowding of a dozen passengers inside, it was as uncomfortable a mode of transport as could be imagined.'

Nonetheless, the newly-weds probably chose the stage coach. That they did so is suggested by the obit's remark that on arriving in Upstate New York they first 'located at Pompey Hill.' Pompey, a small village in the hills above Syracuse, was a stopping point on the stage coach line. The couple could have stayed in Pompey little more than a fortnight for, according to Onondaga County Historical Society micro-film, they next turn up in the 1855 Syracuse census as lodgers under the roof of an emigrant from England near the city centre.

Why settle in Syracuse? The weather there, certainly to the English, was atrocious. Weeks before the arrival of my great-grandfather, the temperature plunged to -30°F or, in English terms, '62 degrees of frost'. A dozen years later Charles Dickens visited the city; he was mightily unimpressed. 'This (Syracuse) is a very grim place in a heavy thaw,' he wrote to Miss Hogarth, his sister-in-law, 'and a most depressing one.'

What was my great-grandfather William to think of his proud new world? Why did he leave England? What was he looking for or, perhaps more importantly, what was he fleeing from? In his obituary in the *Syracuse Post-Standard* of 1904, the photograph depicts an old, if still vigorous, immigrant American. The eyes, deep-set under bushy brows, stare with vague satisfaction at some distant horizon. The mouth is long and hard and below it, obscuring the jaw and part of a dark bow-tie, is a thick, white shovel of a beard, cut in the manner of early American presidents.

As I studied the face, now a century dead, I detected a vexed look creeping into the eyes. Is old William struck by the stench of the photographer's developing fluid? Is he being told to sit still by his son, Isaac Uriah? The wet-plate portrait would have been taken from under a black hood by my grandfather, a commercial photographer.

I return to the text of the obituary. It is peppered with flattery and a hint of a dashing antecedent. William Doust was 'an honored citizen of Syracuse' and a grandson of an officer in the East Indian British Army, writes the obituarist, neglecting to add the family belief that the officer had an arm shot off in some unspecified conflict. Mr Doust, he goes on, was 'employed for many years in the capacity of an engineer at the old Syracuse Iron Works, where he managed the first engine set up in that factory.'

Iron works. The words leap out of the cutting. How odd it seems that my great-grandfather worked in an American iron works in the nineteenth century, whereas his (and my) forebears, Frenchmen from Picardy, are said to have come to England in the early sixteenth century to work in the iron foundries of Sussex. The coincidence strikes me as just that, an intriguing coincidence, and I return to the obituary cutting.

MANAGED THE FIRST ENGINE SYRACUSE IRON WORKS MADE

William Doust, Long a Resident Here, Passes Away at His Home in Richmond Avenue.

WILLIAM DOUST

William Doust, an old-time resident and honored citizen of Syracuse, died at home yesterday at his residence at No. 217 Richmond avenue. Mr. Doust, who was a prominent member of the order of the Hearts of Oak and Onondaga Council No. 61, Royal Arcanum, had been confined to his home for four months with a lingering illness, which ultimately caused his death.

Mr. Doust's career had been an industrious, active and eventful one, filled with successful works. He was a second son of Uriah and Elizabeth Heath Doust, a grandson of an officer in the East Indian British Army and was born November 20, 1833, in Sussex, England. He was married in 1855 to Sarah Green and immediately started for America, making the trip across the Atlantic in a sailing vessel. With his wife he located at Pompey Hill, but came to Syracuse the same year and had resided here ever since. He was employed for many years in the capacity of an engineer at the old Syracuse Iron Works, where he managed the first engine set up in that factory. When this company was discontinued Mr. Doust spent a few months in the mills of Springfield and Chattanooga, returning again to this city as an employe of the Sanderson Bros. Steel Company, now the Crucible Steel Works.

Mr. Doust became a member of the Church of Christ thirty-six years ago and had since been honored with the titles of elder and deacon in that denomination. His wife and family are members of this church and his sons now hold trusted positions in its official departments. During the past twenty years, under the management of his sons, Mr. Doust successfully conducted a grocery business near his home.

Recently the Doust family held a reunion, at which all the members were present and plans were made to hold a jubilee next year in honor of fifty years of wedded life of Mr. and Mrs. Doust. Besides his widow the deceased is survived by I. U., Dr. A. G. and George H. Doust, Mrs. A. J. Kelsey and Dr. H. B. Doust of this city, Sheriff William J. Doust of Spokane county, Wash., Mrs. C. G. Mott of Stroudsburg, Pa., C. E. Doust of Allentown, Pa., and Mrs. M. T. Williams of Kansas City, Mo.

It was a tribute of some 400 words, the only obituary in the paper that day. William had come a long way from being a 'servant' and 'agricultural labourer', the words used to describe him as a 17-year-old in the 1851 census of Udimore, Sussex. What's more, his family's cottage might have been too humble to hold his complete family of two parents and eight brothers and sisters. In the census, William is reported to be living and working at a neighbouring farm.

Picture William, a Sussex teenager, fetching and carrying for room-and-board at another man's farm. Picture him toiling in fields that commanded a beckoning view of the English Channel and the ships plying past. Such ships as the *Simon Taylor*, which nine years earlier had carried his elder brother Isaac and Isaac's family on a 111-day journey of emigration from London to Western Australia. A convincing case indeed can be made out for my great-grandfather casting aside his hoe, marrying a local girl, and setting out for America.

On the other hand, Udimore might have been happy to see the back of the man. By all accounts, William was an awkward cuss. My ageing great-aunt Elinor – who was married to William's autocratic, last-born son, great-uncle 'H.B.' Doust – held this opinion. "I believe William left home because he didn't agree with something that happened in the Church of England," she once told me. "Anyway, he was riled up about something. All Doust men have short tempers at times."

William was certainly riled up in America for, according to one family story, he soon was battling with Episcopal church leaders in Syracuse. So deep was his disenchantment that when he and his wife lost a child in birth, he refused to bury it in the consecrated ground of a cemetery. Instead, he dug a hole in his winter-frozen garden and buried it there. Then he joined the Church of Christ, rose to deacon status and, having reached some kind of spiritual equanimity, gave much thought to the Order of the Hearts of Oak, an English society.

William's Englishness, perhaps refreshed in later life, flowed down through my photographer-grandfather, also a member of the Hearts of Oak. It seeped into my father who, for some reason I never fathomed as a boy, was obsessed with planting oak trees and nut trees in our garden. Oak trees, nut trees and roses. Not so much to enjoy them, I now think, as simply to plant them. It seems as though he was transplanting a little bit of England in Syracuse, New York.

My great-grandfather William, the Father of American Dousts, died at his 'residence' at 217 Richmond Avenue. The street, now less prosperous, is nonetheless generously shaded by trees and its front gardens are tidy. The house has gone. When I visited, the plot was only a long, broad lawn, occupied by a dog house and an Alsatian, which rushed out barking and flung itself against the end of its chain.

"Sheba!" The dog fell silent and a neighbour, a woman perhaps in her sixties, came down off a porch to meet me. Her accent, her round face, immediately gave her away: she's Polish, I thought. This is a Polish part of town. In my day, good high school basketball teams came from here; and an unbidden wave of affection, borne on a smell of cold gyms, swept up from my memory. I must have grinned, for the woman grinned back, and I think this sudden rapport caused me to blurt out: "Did you know a body's buried in your lawn?"

Her face dropped. Hastily, I told her of my great-grandfather. "Buried his own baby?" she said. "That's terrible." I mumbled something like "an odd man", and changed the subject. How long had she lived here? Since the war, she replied. She'd come from Tarnov, a city near Krakow. Why Syracuse? She shrugged and explained that other Poles, friends from Tarnov, had come here before them. She too, I realised, was a 'chain' immigrant. My great-grandparents also had sought comfort among fellow-countrymen in the New World city. I asked the woman if she and her husband were just married when they came to America, like my great-grandparents. She smiled. "No," she said, "that's another story."

What, on the other hand, are we to make of such apparently straightforward place-names as 'Baltonsborough' or 'West Bradley'? If you ask my neighbours for the derivation of these place-names, they'll almost certainly be lost for a precise explanation. However, they'll know in their bones that the names are old – seriously old – and their meanings are rooted deep in the soil round them.

Baltonsborough appears in the Doomsday Book, William the Conqueror's survey of England in 1086, as Baltuneberge. It means 'a small round hill with an enclosure on a larger hill'. This at-first puzzling description holds true as you gaze from my bedroom window: a few fields to the south Baltonsborough is indeed a hill upon a hill.

West Bradley? The name of my hamlet derives from the Old English (sixth to twelfth century) words brad and leah, 'the broad meadow'; and after eight centuries or more, this description also remains accurate. West Bradley lies to the west of a broad meadow which, once again, I can see from my window.

Consider now the mileages on the finger-post. Imagine an American road sign showing all six destinations in fractions. Imagine an American road sign pointing to six places, none farther than eight miles away. It's a small, miniature place, England, where people know their place.

Westbrook House

My English wife and I have lived in Westbrook House for twenty-four years; our two children grew up in the house. The place is part of my life. And yet nothing there – not a figure in a carpet, not a cracked fireplace tile, not a hand-smoothed bannister – triggers a memory. No, that's not true. A stained-glass window at the top of the stairs stirs the memory of a long-ago stained-glass window in my childhood American house.

This recollection is reawakened some mornings when I take our dog from our bedroom down to the kitchen for a biscuit and out the back door for a leg-cock in the fields. The first stop in our ritual journey is at the top of the stairs where Sam bends in a hollow-backed stretch and yawns noisily. Then he rolls on his back, seeking a tummy-scratch. As he rolls, a blade of crimson sunlight ripples across his curly black coat. This trick of light, slanting down from a stained-glass window, picks out something deep in my memory. Only later, as I watch Sam barking down the field, chasing some phantom fox, does the memory grow clear in my mind. I recall 165 Edgehill Road, Syracuse, New York.

It was my first house. Mock-Tudor, its dark-stained front door was fitted with bubbly, stained-glass windows. These windows were alluring, all the more so for being set above my eye-level. To reach them I'd pull up a chair which, even now, I can hear – I can feel – chattering across the tiled vestibule floor. I'd climb on to the chair and peer through the imperfect glass panes: amber, blue, crimson. I'd move my eyes from one pane of glass to another and see the world in its changing moods. Mr Snow's house across the street would, at will, be bathed in a summery orange glow, or cloaked in wintry blue or, snap, set alight in a blaze of licking red flame.

Now, as I waited in my English field, I tested my memory. How many houses could I remember on the opposite side of Edgehill Road? Mr Snow's: white, clapboard, with a green door and a heaving, brick path. Next to Mr Snow – you'll have to take my word for this juxtaposition – came Mr Frost's house. Mr Frost worked for the gas company. That's all I can recall of him. Then came my brother's friend, Jack Welch, who soon died of a heart disease, and then my friend Willie Norris, who once lived in Iowa and later in Florida. Next to Willie, set behind a sloping lawn and perched at the end of the road, stood Bill During's grand house, commanding a grand view over the hills of Syracuse. He was about fifteen.

Bill During. I can't remember what he looked like. Nor have I thought of him in years. But now the name evoked a bitterness, real enough but calloused by time. Here's what I remember. One spring evening, when I was eight or nine, I was in our front garden, pushing round a cart Willie Norris and I had built from an orange crate, two planks and four wheels. My father was clipping his rose bushes when Bill During came sauntering along. As I say, I don't recall what he looked like, but I remember his saunter and what he said to me that day. He admired my orange-crate cart.

He promised he'd help me build an airplane, a real airplane, no bigger than my cart. He himself had once built such an airplane.

He'd worn goggles and flown it round the house tops. He was busy at the moment but, yes, he'd help me build such a plane.

When Bill During left, resuming his saunter down Edgehill Road, my imagination, well, took off. In a glow of excitement I climbed into my cart, which was now an airplane, and tugged on my goggles. I shifted gears (how else would you drive an airplane?), took off, swooped under the telephone cables, narrowly missed Mr Snow's chimney and soared high over Bill During's house and over the edge of the hill. I cut the engine to see better. Below and beyond, a fantasy view opened up: Bradford Hills, where we sledded and ski'd in the winter and, running along the base of the Bradford Hills, the stream called Meadowbrook, where we waded shin-deep to pick cats' tails. Banking my orange-crate airplane, I had begun to follow the wriggling course of the brook when my name was spoken.

It was my father. My fantasy was over. He stood beside me in our front garden, his rose-clippers hanging loose in his hand. He'd heard Bill During. He'd heard the promise. He told me not to get my hopes up. Bill During had only been joking; neither Bill During nor I could build such an airplane. Wasn't Willie Norris's and my orange-crate cart an achievement enough? He tusselled my hair and bet me a nickel Bill During never built an orange-crate cart as nifty as ours.

Now, more than half a century later, I can remember my disillusionment over my orange-crate airplane. I also can remember my satisfaction, untainted by guilt, when later – when I was at university – I heard that Bill During had been killed in an automobile accident.

Bill During wasn't a pleasant memory, I thought that evening as I sat on the stone patio outside Westbrook House. It was a vivid memory, however, and it was my memory. I didn't long for the return of those days, but I remembered the weight of them. Does our West Bradley house stir such odd memories for our daughters?

I can put my finger on the specific moment I realised I was mixing memory and desire. I was in my study, a few springs ago, gazing out at the willow trees lining Bradley Brook, which divides my field from the neighbouring farm. My neighbour's son was pollarding a willow. He was cutting the old limbs back to the trunk with a chain-saw, leaving just the stumps, to allow new shoots to grow strong.

I watched. How many cricket bats, I wondered, could David fashion out of those willows? In my mind, and not for the first time, I rehearsed a few idle cricket strokes: formal little forward-defensive shots, all textbook in perfection. As I opened up with a couple of off-drives, it came to me that over the past dozen years I hadn't thought much about baseball. Willow had replaced hickory in my fantasy.

I had written a good deal about cricket, including three books, but I had never struck a cricket ball in my life. I had never fielded in slips, I realised, and I would have been good at it. Very good, nay a demon. Suddenly, watching a young farmer cut a willow tree, I was lonely for a game I had never played. The pang went deep: here I was, a man past 50, longing for a nostalgia I never knew.

We were an Anglophile household in Edgehill Road, Syracuse. Opposite the fireplace, in front of the couch, *not* the 'sofa', stood the coffee table. On it lay a copy of *The Illustrated London News*. I have no idea how or when it got there but I know it was a souvenir issue commemorating the coronation of George VI. The cover was purple, and embossed with gold lettering which tickled, like Braille print, under my finger-tips. I don't much remember the contents of the magazine – lots of gilded chariots and gun-carriages – but I do recall a photograph of the new king. He was dressed in plus-fours and swinging a golf club. Even then, I could see it wasn't much of a golf swing but I felt treasonous to think so.

Sunday dinner was roast beef, Yorkshire pudding, roast potatoes and two veg, one of them canned peas; and hereby hangs a tale. On the evening of December 7, 1941, a Sunday, we were having dinner, silent in our thoughts of the Japanese attack that day on Pearl Harbour. My father was carving the roast beef when suddenly he set aside the carving knife and brought down his fist on the table. Such was the shuddering force of the blow that the peas leaped out of their bowl and wobbled across my mother's best tablecloth.

A terrified silence re-settled round the table. "The God-damn Prussians!" shouted my father, a man given to shouting, but not profanity. I was confused. I was eleven at the time and knew that Prussians were Germans and, whatever they were now doing in Europe, they hadn't bombed Pearl Harbour.

My father wasn't cruel. He was a doctor, a paediatrician tormented by the suffering of children. In fact, I don't think he forgave God when one died. He worshipped at only one altar: work. Like many of his generation, he hated the Germans; he once told me he returned from World War I with a German soldier's ear pickled in a bottle. I didn't believe him and he never produced it.

As I look back, that dinner on the day of Pearl Harbour takes on a deeper, more symbolic association than war. Afterwards, after America had flexed its muscle, my family seemed to sever its frail links with the home country. Not to put too fine a point on it, after VE Day Americans had an identity of their own: we no longer partook of roast beef and Yorkshire pudding on Sundays. My father died in 1972 and in his obituary photograph, in the *Syracuse Herald-Journal*, he wears a private, impatient smile and a Harris Tweed sport jacket. I now wear the sport jacket.

As the brook trickles out of our lower field, and curls under a tiny, stone bridge, you're struck by a sweet, sickly, smell. It comes from a profuse water plant with masses of flowers, from pink through purple, and dark green leaves. This robust, indeed rampant, annual is called Policeman's Helmet or, more commonly, Himalayan Balsam, or, to the purist, Impatiens glandulifera.

It was brought back to England from the Himalayas by the peripatetic surgeon John Forbes Royle in 1839 and got loose, rather like rabbits in Australia, and went wild along the streams. "A terrorist to botanists," said Sir J.D. Hooker, himself a distinguished Victorian botanist and president of the Royal Society, "deceitful above all plants, and desperately wicked."

Rabbits

Once upon a time – on October 6, 1859, to be exact – twenty-four wild rabbits from Baltonsborough went to sea. They travelled from the Austin house, which you can see across the fields from my house, to Liverpool and from there, via the clipper ship *S.S. Lightning*, to Australia where on Christmas night the ship berthed at Gellibrand's Point, near Melbourne. Off-loaded, they then were delivered to Thomas Austin, who owned an estate called Barwon Park near Geelong in the state of Victoria.

In a manner of speaking, these European rabbits were not the first Austins to be sent to Australia. In 1801, Thomas's uncle James had been convicted of stealing 100 lbs of honey and six bee-hives in Baltonsborough, Somerset, and sentenced to 'transportation beyond the seas for seven years'.

The story behind these modest thefts, and their catastrophic consequences, is legend around Baltonsborough and West Bradley. James Austin, aged 24, and one of five sons, had felt cramped and without prospects on the family farm (he also had four sisters). 'So he made his decision,' J. Marjorie Butler, an Austin descendant, writes in a privately printed book, *Settler by Succession*. 'He would endeavour to get to the new country, Australia, as a convict and there obtain land of his own. "Seven years for Felony" was his only possible escape.'

Accordingly, James and a cousin contrived a harmless "prank". They set six bee-hives outside an uncle's house and shouted for him in the dawn. Answering their call, the hapless uncle stumbled over the hives and was stung. Young Austin and his cousin were duly convicted of 'felonious theft' and, in April 1803, transported with 306 other convicts to Australia on *HMS Calcutta**, a vessel of the Royal Navy.

* Among Austin's fellow convicts was 'Wild White Man' Buckley. In Australia, Buckley escaped into the bush, lived with the aboriginals and, when found thirty years later, had forgotten the English language.

In Australia James thrived and prospered as a sheep farmer, brewer and ferry-boat operator on the River Derwent in Tasmania. Although wealthy, he always 'wore a chip on his shoulder about being a transportee,' according to Mrs Butler, and never married. In 1831 James Austin died without issue and is buried in Tasmania, not far from the settlement he'd nostalgically named 'Baltonsborough Ferry'.

It was his Somerset nephew Thomas, an émigré from Baltonsborough, who in 1859 would summon those twenty-four rabbits from the fields near my house.

Thomas arrived in Van Diemen's Land just after the death of his uncle. He first settled in the Austin properties and then, with his sheep and cattle, crossed the Bass Strait to settle in Victoria, eventually building a grand, bluestone house he called Barwon Park, to where the rabbits were dispatched.

The winters were mild, the fields lush, and the river flowed fresh. What is more, Austin's beloved creatures were being protected like some sort of endangered species: their natural predators – the hawk, the eagle hawk, the feral cat – were systematically slaughtered and, according to another Austin descendant, Austin's gamekeepers 'actually dug holes in the ground for the rabbits because they reckoned their poor little feet wouldn't be able to handle the tough Australian soil.' Not surprisingly, by 1864 Austin's rabbits numbered an estimated 100,000.

In the view of new-settler Thomas, who fancied himself the squire of Barwon Park, the wild rabbits would provide sport in house-party shoots. Indeed, they did. According to a contemporary issue of *The Field* magazine, a kill of 14,253 rabbits was reported at Barwon Park in 1867. In the same year another staggering kill was banged off when Austin entertained Prince Alfred, Queen Victoria's second son, whom she had just made the Duke of Edinburgh. 'In about three and a half hours the party killed 4,000-odd rabbits, of which the Duke shot 416,' recounted another family historian, Mrs R.A. Austin, OBE, JP, who failed to question the Duke's kill-rate of two rabbits a minute. In the same year, Thomas Austin was honoured by the Australian Acclimatisation Society for bringing the little beasts to the continent.

It was the wild rabbits which got away from Barwon Park that were to become prominent in the annals of animal pestilence. These rabbits, many-generation descendants of Baltonsborough's twenty-four European *Oryctolagus cuniculus*, were to lay waste the countryside of a nation in the Rabbit Plague that began in Australia in the late nineteenth century.

How the rabbits escaped Austin's estate is unclear. A Barwon River flood may have knocked over the paling fence round the paddocks containing them. Or the fences may have rotted out or, as Mrs Austin, writing nearly a century later in *The Victorian Historical Magazine*, stoutly contended: 'the people of Winchelsea (a local village) did not see why they should not have rabbits, too, so they broke the enclosure and the rabbits took charge of Australia.'

In any event, the ravenous rabbits, nine of which could eat as much as one sheep, nibbling all before them, multiplying mercilessly, travelling at an estimated rate of 110 kilometres a year, headed northwards across Victoria, New South Wales and Queensland. They munched westwards through South Australia and swept wave upon wave across the Nullarbor Plain. 'In theory, it is possible for a single pair of rabbits to have produced 62,064 descendants by the end of their third season,' wrote John Vandenbeld in *Nature of Australia*.

A rabbit fence 1,139 miles long – a distance twice the length of Britain – was stretched across Western Australia, taking six years to build. It did little good. The rabbits broke through and under it and by 1894 they were swarming across the vast western state. Three years later they reached the Indian Ocean at Geraldton, more than 200 miles north of Perth and perhaps 2,500 roundabout miles from the Austin estate at Barwon Park. 'Eventually, the rabbit spread to the desert and the snow-clad mountains,' one historian wrote poetically. 'It has overrun half the continent.'

Not until after the Second World War, when the Australian rabbit population had reached an estimated 1,000 million, was the plague properly tackled.

For this, the shamed Austin family took some credit. 'I have always felt that, as Austins brought the successful (sic) rabbits to Australia, so Austins should help to destroy them,' Mrs R.A. Austin wrote in her magazine article. 'That is one reason why I did everything I could and used every opportunity available to me to help the campaign to get myxomatosis going in 1950-53.' The introduced virus disease, she went on, was to be 'the salvation of the pastoral lands of Australia … in a battle which resulted in the extermination of at least 200 million rabbits.'

In 1987, a century after the onset of Australia's rabbit plague, I was in Melbourne to cover the Australian Open tennis championship for *The Sunday Times* of London. At the time I was well aware of Baltonsborough's connection with the rabbit plague and, planning one day to write about it, I found 'T. Austin' in the Geelong phone book.

I dialled and introduced myself as a journalist from England, "actually from Somerset". At the other end of the line Tom Austin groaned in mock despair. "Oh dear, I suppose you want to talk about rabbits," he said, affably enough. "I'll be up at Kooyong (then the site of the championship) for the tennis tomorrow." He gave me his seat and section number. "See you there."

The next day Austin, a big, friendly, athletic-looking man, handed me his card as we watched Boris Becker polishing off the Yugoslav Bobo Zivojinovic in the third round of the championship. As the players changed ends, I studied the card:

The Hon. Tom Austin, MP
Deputy Leader Liberal Parliamentary Party
Parliament of Victoria
Member for Ripon
Shadow Minister for Agriculture

Shadow Minister for Agriculture. It seemed too good to be true. Austin, I realised, would be the Liberal spokesman on rabbit affairs. Indeed, later, as we sat under Kooyong's famous sign-post pointing to Wimbledon, he said: "In the last Liberal state government, when I was the Minister for Agriculture, I was never allowed to forget those bloody rabbits my great-grandfather brought into the country. When I rose to speak, the Opposition would shout 'Bunny, Bunny, Bunny!'"

A prosperous farmer himself, Austin had until recently raised sheep and a few cattle on his 1,600-acre farm near Geelong. He had learned to shoot on the family farm when he was a boy. "Rabbiting, that was how most Australians learned to shoot. It was great sport, either killing the rabbit to eat or just for a bit of fun. We used to put ferrets down the burrows and shoot the rabbits as they came running out."

Austin went into the Australian navy during the war. "Afterwards," he explained, "I actually made my living trapping rabbits on a farm west of here, in Ballarat. I was setting over one hundred traps and catching thirty pairs a night. I'd send them down to a delicatessen in Footscray, a suburb of Melbourne. That's how I learned to skin rabbits. We hold the World Rabbit-Skinning Championships."

Austin warmed to the memory. "You'd take the dead rabbit, chop off its tail, gut it and skin it. The skinning itself took only about ten or twelve seconds, but you had to be careful; you weren't allowed to damage the pelt. Then you'd hang up the rabbit for the judges to examine. When I was going along well, I could do three rabbits in a minute." Austin had once reached the finals of the championship, he said, losing to the great 'Killer' Crawford, the Don Bradman of rabbit-skinning.

He recalled the day. It was Boxing Day, and hot. He himself had opened the festivities, dressed in a dark suit, collar and tie. He'd competed, dressed in a dark suit, collar and tie. He chuckled. No, he wouldn't have won if he'd been dressed in a swim suit. 'Killer' Crawford was too good. Crawford was unbeatable, until years later when his hands seized up with arthritis. Austin grinned and said, "I think that's enough of rabbit-talk for a while. Let's go watch the tennis."

In the stands we sat in sunshine as Becker completed his victory and Ivan Lendl won his match. It was all good stuff, I suppose, but my thoughts were stuck on that rabbit-skinning championship. In my mind, I pictured Tom Austin bent over a rabbit, furiously chopping, gutting and skinning. I watched his armpits grow dark with sweat as he fought to repair the damage his great-grandfather had done to Australia, by creating Watership Down Under.

Mells and Glastonbury

The shallow valley where the Austin rabbits once played is overlooked from the north by a modest ridge which, since Domesday, has been known as Worms Hill. It was down this ridge, according to the Perambulation of the Glastonbury XII Hides, published in 1509, that an entourage of men and boys, perhaps as many as forty, made their way on the afternoon of July 26, 1503.

The group almost certainly moved sluggishly. Only moments before they had stopped at a gate, near where the British Gas Corporation's pipeline valves now stand. According to Brother Sutton, the chronicler of the Glastonbury XII Hides, 'Lord Abbot and all the rest of the company then and there present made a light meal of bread, beer, and wine etc.' What is more, they would have been tired; they'd already done a dozen miles since morning and still had thickly wooded Pennard Hill to climb on their 65-mile journey round the boundary of the Church's Twelve Hides.

On their walk their purpose was to note down 'little details of the lands, fields, pastures, plantations and forests' and, accordingly, to determine who owed what tithe to the Church. Richard Bere, the penultimate Abbot of Glastonbury, led the way. Bere was an Oxonian, friend of the great Renaissance humanist Erasmus, and Henry VII's emissary to the Pope.

With him strode 'trusty John Horner, surveyor' who, adroitly swirling his measuring chain, made his way down off Worms' Hill, past my neighbour's – David Cotton's – present barnyard, over the stream, through my fields and on into history. There, his name is embedded in perhaps the most famous of all nursery rhymes:

Little Jack Horner
Sat in a corner,
Eating a Christmas pie.
He put in his thumb,
Pulled out a plum
And said, what a good boy am I.

I visited Horner's descendant, the 2nd Earl of Oxford and Asquith. He was not much amused by the nursery rhyme's coded allusion. "I don't give much credence to that legend," he said at the Manor House in Mells, a village in the north of Somerset. We were sitting in the drawing-room of the house, a much-restored Elizabethan building that represents the 'plum' in the nursery rhyme. It had been owned since the Dissolution of the Monasteries by the Horner family – Lord Oxford's mother had been a Horner – and he was well-versed, indeed soaked, in the story. No, Lord Oxford and Asquith insisted over a glass of sherry, Mells was purchased by the Horners from Henry VIII.

The 'trusty John Horner, surveyor' appears to me anything but trusty. A small man, said in one fable to have been descended from a dwarf thirteen inches tall, Horner was also ingratiating and ambitious. At the time of the Dissolution, when Glastonbury Abbot Richard Whiting sought to bribe Henry VIII, Horner was chosen to carry a great Christmas plum pie to the king, as a gesture of appeasement.

In this pie were hidden the title deeds to twelve Benedictine manors. While en route to London in a carriage Horner, the story goes, put his thumb into the pie and pulled out the deeds to Mells Manor. 'However this may be,' write Iona and Peter Opie in their definitive *Oxford Dictionary of Nursery Rhymes*, 'it is a fact that one Thomas Horner took up residence at Mells soon after the Dissolution and his descendants live there to this day.'

Lord Oxford is the grandson of the Liberal Prime Minister Herbert Asquith. He is the nephew of Lieutenant Edward Horner, who was the last direct male heir to Little Jack Horner. Of his infamous forebear, Lieut Horner, who died of wounds suffered in action during World War I, wrote home to Mells as an Eton schoolboy: 'My name is already a curse to me.'

In Mells' church, Edward Horner is honoured by an equestrian statue by Sir Alfred Munnings. I'm drawn to the churchyard where Siegfried Sassoon, a university-days hero of mine, is buried. I resist wandering after *that* story. To follow a line of English history, I'm learning, is seductive: once you pick it up, it's hard to let go. I return to my brook.

Back to the brook

I saw a heron standing on one leg in a field. Presently it raised its head from between its shoulders, looked about and, lifting off, lumbered low through the air, its legs trailing awkwardly behind. The heron flew over the hawthorn hedges and low under the red plastic balls that dangle from wires strung between electricity pylons. A heron might not fly as gracefully as a swan, but he doesn't need 'swan balls' to warn him off bumping into electric wires.

The plastic balls resembled ball-cocks but, in fact, they were fishing floats, colloquially called 'swan balls' or, more properly, 'bird-flight diverters'. Western Power Distributors had hung them on their wetland wires since the 1970s, reducing the swan fatalities from scores to three or four a year on the Levels. "Of all the wetland birds, the swans need the most help," a company official would tell me. "Their eyes are on the sides of their heads, you see, so their forward vision is not so good. What's more, they're heavy birds, and not very manoeuvrable. They don't exactly swoop round like house martins."

In the same field I saw, too, a scattering of sheep's wool, looking like a patch of dirty spring snow. "Belly wool. Rubbish." So the farmer, Bob Cotton, told me later. "Sheep shearers just chuck it away." The previous summer the sheep-shearers had visited Cotton's farm. They were part of the wave of itinerant agricultural farm-workers who travel annually to Britain from the Southern Hemisphere.

The following June, a new team of shearers came to the farm. What a racket. A cacophony of penned-up, bleating sheep, a ghetto-blasting radio, turned high to *Radio One,* and the click and whine of electric clippers led me to Cotton's silage shed. The team was made up of a pair of tall, lean young shearers dressed in singlets, jeans and custom-built mocassins, coated with an accumulation of sheep dust: Jimmy Allsop, a shepherd from New Zealand's sheep-strewn South Island, and the Falkland Islander John McKay, whose initials, tattooed in Japanese, covered the whole of his forearm. "No, I've never been to Japan," he shouted over the din. "The tattoos were done back home by a Chilean."

The team's third member was a cheerful, bustling little girl-woman from the Falklands called Tracey Evans. I watched as she scooped up a fleece from the floor, flung it on to an improvised table, wrapped it like so much laundry and bundled it into a white builders' merchant's bag. She rested a moment and grinned. "I'm a roustabout," she said. "A rousie. In the old days men were the rousies. Now it's a woman's job." She kept her eyes on the shearers, poised to pounce on the next fleece.

It's hard, sheep-wrestling work, leavened by the satisfaction of flashes of artful clipper-play. First, eight or ten sheep are driven tightly into a 'catch-pen'. The shearers enter through flap-doors, catch a sheep and shear it. At the end of the day's work, which stretched from 10 a.m. to 9 p.m., a total of 550 sheep and 15 rams had been shorn. Farmer Cotton was satisfied. The fleeces, after grading by the British Wool Marketing Board, would go into carpets, bedding and insulation materials and, said Cotton, "just about paid for the shearing". As for the shearing team, they too were satisfied. A total of 550 sheep and 15 double-click* rams meant 580 units, multiplied by 65 pence, which equals £337. They were off next day to a farm on the Mendip Hills.

> * Editor's note: the shearing of a ram is recorded by two clicks on the counter.

On the ridge of the Polden Hills above the hamlet of Butleigh Wootton, I saw a slender column, the Hood monument. It commemorates Admiral Samuel Hood* (1724-1816) who, like his younger brother Admiral Alexander Hood (1726-1814), distinguished himself in naval battles. Why these men, born in inland Butleigh, should have been drawn to the sea is explained in a family story.

> * Editor's note: Most confusingly the monument is actually dedicated to Sir Samuel Hood (1762-1814), a second cousin from Dorset. He too had a brother Alexander, and like their older cousins they were both distinguished naval commanders. Alexander's wife was from Butleigh, and she had the monument erected.

One winter day in 1740, a carriage carrying a Royal Navy captain from Plymouth to London broke down in Butleigh. With no inn at hand, the Vicar of Butleigh, the Reverend Hood, invited the captain to stay at the vicarage. There, round an evening fire, the guest enchanted the young Hoods with tales of the sea.

The Royal Navy captain offered to take the boys to sea. Alexander, aged 13, went straightaway and Samuel soon followed. When yet another, younger, brother sought to answer the call, his parents intervened. "Two of our boys will be drowned," they protested. "We cannot spare a third." The boy stayed at home and, while still young, drowned in the River Brue not far from the vicarage.

This tragedy would not be the last drowning to be associated with the name of Hood in British history. That tragedy, almost exactly two hundred years later, would befall 'Britain's mightiest warship', the battle cruiser *HMS Hood* of 21,921 tons. Destroyed by the German battleship *Bismarck*, the *Hood* would go down in the icy waters between Iceland and Greenland on May 24, 1941, carrying with her all but three of her 1,421 crew.

The stream flowed under Cox Bridge; it had picked up Coxbridge Brook, and together they trundled west. So did I. Passing Bob Cotton's sixteenth century farmhouse, I was tempted to knock on the door and have a look at his Elizabethan circular staircase – Nell, our youngest daughter, once sketched it for a school art project – but the temptation passed and I kept walking. In a moment I was on Kennard Moor, an eastern gateway to the Somerset Levels, some 250 square miles of what makes up the largest marshland area on the west coast of Britain.

The view opened up round me. Off to the northwest, maybe a mile away, Glastonbury Tor rose out of the flat landscape. The mood of the Tor depends on the weather, and today was bright and cloudy. A light breeze chased cloud shadows across the rippling slopes of the strange hill while, at the top, tiny figures moved round the ruined stone tower. I looked for cows. I always look for cows when I see the Tor.

This habit was planted in my mind by Dick House, a moors farmer. For years, House farmed 325 acres on the moor and he once told me a local saying: "If there are cows on the Tor, it's either fair weather or it's *going* to be fair weather." What about no cows? What did that mean? Involuntarily, my attention was drawn back to the land round my feet.

Something odd was going on down there. I was walking above the surrounding fields, five or six feet above them. I was on a 'high water carrier', an embankment, sort of a mini-Mississippi levee, without the sand bags. Beneath me the stream, now a dozen feet across, had become an artificial waterway and would remain an artificial waterway for the rest of its twenty-odd miles to the sea. A millennium ago the sea was here, but successive drainage projects, begun by twelfth century Glastonbury monks, have turned it into grassland, ruled off by straight drainage ditches, or 'rhynes', and bordered by hawthorn hedges. Sheep grazed in the flat pastures.

Flat pastures? Not quite flat for, looking closely, I saw the pastures rippling in long, low ridges. Under each ridge ran a 'gripe' which, *Black's Agricultural Dictionary* tells us, is a 'small ditch or furrow used to drain surface water off grassland.' These gripes appeared uniformly spaced, so I dropped off the embankment and paced them off: they were 11 yards apart, an intriguing distance.

A chain is a centuries-old measuring tool for surveyors. Its length is 22 yards and, as Dick House put it, "just long enough to turn round a team of ploughing oxen." I'm no mathematician, but I could work out that 11 yards is exactly half the distance needed to turn round a team of oxen. So how did the ploughman plough in his extra furrow?

The Tor

Glastonbury Tor is owned by the National Trust, which has placed a perspex-covered tablet at the base of that strange lump of earth. 'Tor is a West Country word of Celtic origin meaning a hill,' it begins. The message then goes on to knock dead the romantic notion that the hill is man-made. 'Glastonbury Tor is a natural formation composed of layers of clay and blue limestone, capped by a mass of hard, erosion-resistant sandstone.'

The Tor's top is 518 feet above sea level, the tablet goes on. 'The tower is all that remains of the medieval church of St Michael, built by the Abbey to replace a previous church which fell in an earthquake in the 13th century.' Excavations of the summit area have revealed traces of a much earlier building, dating from the fifth or sixth century A.D.

'The terraces running round the hillside are in their present form strip lynchets, fields of a medieval type, whatever they may conceal,' the inscription went on. 'The Tor is and has been to many people a place of magic, the focus of legend and superstition. There is a current theory that the terraces formed a sort of three-dimensional maze. One local story is that there is a hollow space inside; another, perhaps very ancient, that the hill has a secret entrance to the Underworld.

'The Tor was the scene of the hanging, drawing and quartering of Richard Whiting, the last Abbot of Glastonbury, when Henry VIII dissolved the Abbey in 1539.'

The path curls upwards, as if in a fairy tale, towards the stone tower and the sky. The climb, while strenuous for the aged and unfit, is hugely popular: 250,000 visitors are said to make it each year. More likely, the statistic is 250,000 climbs are made each year, for many Glastonians toil, or run, up it. Still, as I paused to rest on a bench midway into the eastern ascent, I reckoned that however you measure it, a quarter of a million was a lot of climbs per year. That makes nearly 5,000 a week, nearly 700 a day. Nearly what? Thirty an hour! Night and day. Winter and summer. Rain or shine. Indeed, Glastonbury maketh myths.

One Tor story that decidedly isn't a myth concerns the last ascent by the luckless Abbot Whiting in 1539. In the autumn of that year he was taken from his hunting lodge at Sharpham, out on the Levels, by Henry VIII's mounted commissioners. Bundled away to Wells for trial, the frail old cleric was found guilty of treason, returned to Glastonbury, lashed on to a sheep hurdle and, together with two fellow monks, hauled by horse to the top of the Tor.*

* For the steep ascent, Henry's men might better have improvised the device used in 1948 by Cribb & Sons, the Glastonbury builders, when the tower was renovated. Materials were loaded on to a cart made with small wheels in front and big ones behind. Ropes and pulleys were strung over the Tor's summit and attached to a horse. The horse then was led down the far side, pulling the now-horizontal cart up the steep slope.

There, on 15 November, Whiting was hanged, beheaded and his body hacked into four parts. His head was impaled on the gate of Glastonbury Abbey, his four parts taken for display in Wells, Bridgwater, Ilchester and Bath. Then, as further warning to Catholics, the three gallows were left standing on the Tor for people to see from miles around.

From my bench I gazed north to the BBC's television tower, thin as a thermometer, on a distant hill above Wells. Would the BBC have covered the abbot's trial? And, yielding to the king's wishes, filmed the execution?

I carried on up the curling path and suddenly the tower of St Michael's loomed over me. And there, behind a buttress and out of the cold, buffeting wind, sat a man on a blanket. He wore a Peruvian smock, jeans and the kind of broad, red shoes that are hand-made in Glastonbury. Beside him, within touching distance, lay a magnificent rack of stag antlers.

The man's name turned out to be equally magnificent: Rod St Barbe. His surname, he told me, was adopted by his forebears generations ago in honour of St Barbe, a sainted Barbary Coast nun. He himself was Cornish-born but he'd come to Glastonbury in 1945 at the age of three days. "My mum wanted me to be brought up in the Druid tradition," he said, "so she sent me to my grandparents who were Druids living in Glastonbury."

Apart from a few recent years in North Devon, where his brief marriage foundered and where he'd found the antlers during his eighty-mile walk away from his marriage, St Barbe had lived in Glastonbury ever since. He once had a foundry in town where he hammered out replica antique swords for the use of 're-enactment people' round the world. Broadswords, sabres, cutlasses, whippy little rapiers. He'd had a go at the lot.

When the sword business went bust, St Barbe built and sold kites, their unique designs based on "the body shapes of falcons" that he'd watched feathering and falling through the restless air round the Tor. Indeed, the Tor had played a big part in his boyhood. As well as flying those kites above it, he'd swum in the dark, cold waters beneath it.

Beneath the Tor? He smiled and explained. "Down near where the path starts up the hill," he said, gesturing towards the path I'd taken, "there used to be a hole the size of a large badger hole. It slanted into the ground. We'd slide down it and into an underground lake. We'd swim and dive down. But we never found the bottom.

"In the Fifties, two pot-holers went down," he went on. "When they came out they were bonkers. Stark-raving mad. Ended up in the asylum at Wells." Since then, the hole has been collared in concrete and covered by a padlocked metal lid. Was this the fabled entrance to the Underworld? St Barbe said no. "That's over on the south side. It's blocked by a big, egg-shaped rock. Some say King Arthur is asleep down there."

St Barbe knew his Tor. In fact, he not only was an unofficial Tor guide, sharing his eccentric wisdom with tourists, but did a bit of Energy Healing on the Tor. "One day this old man came staggering up the Tor with his wife," he recounted. "He looked awful. White as a sheet. He said he had heart trouble. So I sat him down on my blanket and when he'd got his breath, I helped him up and took him round and stood him on the node."

The node?

"That's where the ley lines cross. I know. I've dowsed it," he said. The wind had got up and, making his way through it, he walked to a spot. "I stood him here and, right away, I could see something was wrong. I asked his wife if he had cancer in his left side. She said he did. Which was obvious. His whole left side was tipped over because the earth's energy was pulling the cancer out of his body. I had him stand there for half an hour. And afterwards, he was absolutely dancing." St Barbe paused. "All medicine is energy, you see. And in Earth Healing, you're going back to the purest form of energy, the earth."

Ill-equipped to dispute this, I asked St Barbe if he had any idea where the gallows had been placed for Abbot Whiting and his two mates in 1539. He did. "Tourists often picnic up here on the Tor and if they sit over there," he said, indicating a place near where we stood, "they don't like it. They get up and move. There's something uncomfortable about the place."

A group of tourists appeared around a turn in the path and St Barbe seemed eager to meet them. I thanked him for his time, tipped him, and roamed down and round the crest of the Tor. On the south side, I found the entrance to the Underworld: a limestone boulder among badger setts and under a hawthorn tree. New Age travellers had made a shrine of the site. The tree was decorated with red, purple and yellow ribbons, one limb encrusted in glass crystals. The date '17.2.48' was carved into the limestone boulder.

Briefly, I imagined King Arthur asleep under this kitsch and, briefly, I imagined Abbot Richard Whiting dangling from his gallows and turning in the wind some 450 years ago. What clung in my mind, however, was the picture of Rod St Barbe walking out of his marriage, walking across rolling Exmoor towards Glastonbury. What drew him back to the town, what comfort might he have gained in finding those stag antlers?

From the Tor, you can gaze down over Glastonbury (population 9,500), the best-known town of its size in Britain. The reason for its fame, a symbol of its mystical power, is easy to pick out. There, silhouetted against the sky on Wearyall Hill, is a tiny, wind-bent hawthorn tree. It's a descendant of the thorn tree said to have sprung from the staff that Joseph of Arimathea plunged into the soil when he carried Christianity to Britain in the first century.

If the citizens of Glastonbury were to choose a banner to lead them into the next millennium, they could do worse than put the hawthorn tree on it. Perhaps a thorn tree on a field of black, the black of a Safeway car park that lies below the tree, for these images represent the conflict that keeps the town vital.

'Every town is special, if only in some respects,' the Londoner David Williams writes in *A Glastonbury Community Plan*, his 1996 report to the Civic Trust. 'But Glastonbury is unique.'

Bradley Brook turned a very sharp left toward its rendezvous with the Brue.

I turned right down Cinammon Lane in the lea of the Tor and almost straightaway ran into a flock of sheep. It moved along the lane in a soft, muffled clatter of hooves, while a pair of sheep dogs darted about, heads low, hurrying the animals. Up ahead a farm woman led the way on a wobbly bicycle while the shepherd followed behind. A short, wiry man, suddenly friendly, he apologised for clogging up the lane.

"Taking the sheep up the Tor," he said and, over the next ten minutes or so, he dropped back now and then for a chat. His name was Ron Fouracres. "We was always told we're of Saxon, or maybe Roman, stock and this is what we heard," he said, his voice dropping in conspiracy, his accent round as a Somerset apple. "Story is, we was rewarded with four acres of land because we did such a good job fightin' for the Saxons, or maybe it was for the Romans." He chuckled. "That's why the name were created and that's why, if you look through, most of the Fouracres has always got a farming background."

He invited me to his bungalow over the hill on Leg of Mutton Road, a suitable address for a shepherd in fabled Glastonbury. By the hearth stood a heavy iron doorstop, in the form of a woolly sheep. On the wall hung the photograph of an alert, hard-panting sheepdog. Ron said her name was Bess and that she'd been stolen some years ago. Sheep and dogs are never far from sight in the Fouracres world. There are ten Glastonbury Fouracres listed in the residential section of the local phone book and, according to the ready-reckoning June Fouracres, Ron's book-keeper wife, something like forty of them live in or around town.

In lambing time, or when they are dipping their sheep, Ron and June and their dogs, Jeff and Gus, bring the flock up from the sheds they have on the moors. They pass Honeysuckle House, once the Fouracres's family farmhouse, climb Cinnamon Lane, cross the busy A361 – "I stop the traffic," June chipped in, "Ron and the dogs look after the sheep" – and with the sound of Ron's sharp whistle cutting through the sheep's soft, hurrying hoof-clatter, they carry on up Well House Lane to the slopes of the Tor.

There, Fouracres has tacked up a crude, emphatic, handwritten sign, 'Sheep Grazing. Please Keep Your Dogs on Leads'. His words are a cri de coeur, for he's devoted to his flock and over the years it has been savaged and depleted by dogs on the Tor. "A while back," he explained, "when I was foolish enough to put the sheep up there on weekends, we lost sixteen – sixteen in a year."

In most other years, he'd lost half-a-dozen. Only a month ago, due to harassing dogs, he said, his vet's bill was £158.00 for medicine and surgical patch-ups. His annual £980 grazing contract with the National Trust ran out soon and he doubted he would renew it. "It's good grazing, mind, beautiful grazing. Animals been grazing up there for centuries. But what can I do? We've lost enough to say enough's enough." He paused. "That's why you didn't see my sheep on the Tor. We've had them off since April the first."

There was no self-pity, only puzzlement and no little anger in his voice. "The killer mostly is stress, especially in young lambs," he explained. "If you see 'em on the Tor with no dogs about they're as contented as can be. They'll lie down, maybe for four hours, doing themselves some good and doing me some good. But let dogs loose, or put them on one of them thirty-feet extension leads, and the sheep'll be constantly on the move. Over there one minute. Over there the next. Over the other side."

He lived in dread of phone calls telling of dead sheep on the Tor. "You bet your life it'll be a lamb," he said. "Got itself all stressed up and dropped dead." He went on to tell of how loose dogs go for the hind legs of a sheep, throw it down and attack the underbelly. He told how he once put prized Dorset Horn sheep on the Tor. "Right away, they got chased by a dog. Ran so fast they fell and rolled down the hill. Broke their legs. Broke their horns off. Blood all over the place."

June Fouracres intervened to tell of a recent, hot summer day. A family of a dozen tourists, picnicking round a water trough on the Tor, unwittingly kept the timid sheep from the trough. "The family just didn't know. And when we asked them to move off," she said, "the sheep came up like a herd of thirsty elephants." Then Ron told of New Age travellers camping near a trough that got so dirty with crystals and candle wax, soap and dog hairs, that the sheep wouldn't touch the water.

What was the solution? "I don't know," he admitted. "But the problem's too many people on the Tor these days. And too many dogs, even on leads." I persisted: what was the solution? After a moment, Ron said, "No sheep at all on the Tor." He cocked his jaw. "But, with no sheep to graze it, the Tor's going to go back, get full of weeds. It's going to get rough and untidy."

Plainly, in Fouracres's view, there was no solution to the demands of modern-day life. There wasn't much more to say. As I left the bungalow, I glanced at the photograph of Bess, his stolen sheepdog. "Did the travellers nick her?" I asked. "No," said Ron, "you can't blame the travellers for everything."

The Chalice Well, at the western foot of the Tor, takes the Joseph of Arimathea legend one step further. Joseph is said to have brought more than a staff from the Holy Land. In among his baggage was the Holy Grail, or Chalice Cup, from which Jesus drank 'at the last sad supper', according to Tennyson in his Arthurian *Idylls of the King*.

Joseph is said to have buried the cup in the Chalice gardens. It has not been found, unsurprisingly, but the well has a literary connection. A pipe gushes water into the street. The novelist Henry Fielding once drank it and found it – as I did – of 'a sulphurous and steely quality'. Fielding died soon afterwards in Portugal.

Welcome to Glastonbury

At the western foot of the Tor, built into a hill, stood a modern glassy house on Well House Lane, its walls painted a peaceful pale blue. A tidy sign introduced

Berachah House
En-suite Accommodation
Colour Healing Centre
Colour Healing Aura Soma
Aura Soma Massage Astrology
&
Hand Painted Silks

It might have added 'Welcome to Glastonbury', for here was the first commercial establishment catering to the alternative society. 'Berachah', I later would learn, means 'a place of special spiritual blessing' and the house itself 'holds transforming energy'. Tapping into such energy at Berachah, however, didn't come cheap: Aura Soma, or 'in-depth colour reading', cost £25 an hour, or £35 if you followed it up with a massage with appropriately selected coloured oils.

I explained my limited resources to the proprietress, a shy and friendly Welsh woman called Jan Billings, and she offered to demonstrate colour reading free of charge. We climbed the stairs and walked down a hall past the Green Room (double, en-suite, with breakfast, £45 a night) and the Blue Room (single etc, £25) and into Ms Billings' consulting room.

The near wall was stunning: it was made up of shelf upon shelf of coloured bottles. I sat on the floor and counted eight rows of twelve bottles; in all, ninety-six bottles. Each bottle, what's more, contained two fluids of different colours. "The oil is in the top half of the bottle, the water in the bottom half," Ms Billings said. "The colours are the basic spiritual colours. Violet, indigo, blue, green, yellow, orange, red." The arrangement looked like a carefully artless modern painting.

"In a reading, I ask you to choose five bottles," Ms Billings began. "The first bottle represents your mission in this life." Her slight emphasis on the words 'in this life' unsettled me. Did I have a mission in another life? "The second bottle represents your past," she went on. "The third your present. The fourth your future, just round the corner. The fifth your ultimate goal, at this point in time."

Your future, just round the corner. Your ultimate goal, at this point in time. The qualifiers were coming too thick and fast for me. I needed time to stop and consider them. "Just for the fun of it," she continued, "let's examine one bottle, your 'mission in life' bottle." She opened her hands towards the wall: I was to choose a bottle.

Without a thought, I picked one from the far side of the bottom row. Bright red above bright green. Ms Billings nodded. "That is called the Robin Hood bottle," she said. "It is about infectious enthusiasm for life. The red represents your physicality – your passion, your sexuality, your anger. The green, on the other hand, represents your peace and well-being, your heart. So now we've established your balance between the red and the green."

What if I chose a green-over-red bottle? I wondered. Ms Billings smiled; she plainly knew her bottles. "Green over red. That means you have difficulty assessing your energy," she said. I pictured the colours green over red, and the image of inverted traffic lights came to mind. Maybe, I suggested, when motorists see green over red they have trouble assessing their energies. Maybe it is safer to hang traffic lights red over green. Like a Robin Hood bottle.

Just then, a bell rang somewhere in the house. "Can I let two people into their room?" She broke off. "I'll get you the Robin Hood print-out to look at while I'm away." She disappeared, returned with the print-out and disappeared again to answer the bell. I studied the print-out. It began:

'Name of bottle: Robin Hood'. Then, 'Colour: Red/Green'. Then, 'Shakes Together As: Red'. Further down, my 'I Ching sign' seemed fitting, if over-dramatic in this stage of my journey down an English stream: 'Mountain Above, Thunder Below.' Further, in Positive Personality Aspects, I was 'Someone with courage and heart, who dares to push forward into the unknown.'

Good stuff, very insightful. Spiritual Level? 'Encourage the user to give space for the soul to unfold.' Where to Apply the Substance? 'Around the entire trunk.' Affirmation? 'I see the light through the trees.' And in conclusion, Distinctive Qualities? I read the print-out. I re-read it, surprised. I've got an open mind. Anyone has a right to his or her opinion, even a print-out. But this one didn't know me. It said, in part:

"This combination ... often shows that the person is about to go through a separation or divorce ... This substance helps a person to handle their trans-sexuality ..." A person, their trans-sexuality? I chuckled to myself. Such bad grammar threw my entire personality assessment into doubt. I no longer fancied a massage 'around the entire trunk' with red and green oils.

When Ms Billings returned, she seemed preoccupied with her forthcoming chores, tidying up the Green Room perhaps, or dusting her bottles of oil and water. I was keeping her from her work. It was time to go, to push forward into the unknown, so to speak. I thanked her for her generosity in giving me a brief run-down on colour therapy. It was all very interesting and, I was sure, very helpful to those in distress.

At the door I paused to ask one last question. Why, I wondered, was the red-over-green bottle called a 'Robin Hood' bottle? Could it be that red and green were the colours of Robin Hood's costume? Ms Billings laughed. "The green-over-green bottle is the 'Go-Hug-A-Tree' bottle," she said brightly.

I took Chilkwell Street, an extension of the A361, into the town Ron Fouracres affectionately called 'crystal and candle wax'. On the street side of the raised pavement stood an iron railing; on the other a row of attached cottages, parts of which dated back to the seventeenth century. As a boy, Fouracres had known everyone who lived in these houses, now he knew none. Window stickers told the story. In one, Lord Kitchener, wagging his famous finger, exclaimed: 'The World Needs You. Go Organic Now.' Another supported a yoga workshop in Glastonbury, a third declared 'Angels at Work. Prepare for Miracles'.

Strung out along the railings were ten wooden tubs, each sprouting a young tree. The trees not only were part of the Glastonbury in Bloom scheme but, I suspected, would one day blot up noise and fuel pollution that poured mercilessly from passing lorries.

It is tempting to think that Glastonbury has the highest percentage of non-native residents of any town in England: as in the case of the Barton family from Newcastle. I asked Jo-Jo, the *Big Issue* salesman by the war memorial, rising above the pavement outside St John's Church, if he had known Robert Barton. "No," he said, "but Liz, his mother, will tell you about him. Her office is above the 'Truckle of Cheese'." Jo-Jo, a latecomer to town, probably didn't know Robert Barton. But, like almost everyone else in and around Glastonbury, he knew about Robert Barton, the victim in one of the most poignant tragedies among the town's travellers.

Barton, a guitar-playing, would-be juggler and cider-drinking member of the bench-dwellers, had died on Saturday, September 21, 1996. The death of any Glastonbury 'hippy' excites interest in the community and *The Central Somerset Gazette* carried the story on its front page. It ran under the headline, 'Death of a 'Gentle Boy'.

'An extraordinary display of sorrow followed the death of 21-year-old Robert Barton in Glastonbury,' the story began. 'Friends of the member of the town's alternative community placed his guitar in the middle of chalked messages and covered the spot alongside the town's war memorial with flowers.

'His body was found on Sunday morning at a flat at Church Path alongside St John's Church where his stunned friends attended Evensong later. The Reverend Patrick Riley said, "I think it is people's longing to find some way of expressing what they feel. He was a very gentle boy."

'Sgt Judy Hanchet said the police were awaiting the results of the post-mortem. Hours after his death, Robert was expected to make a court appearance at Wells for a sentence on offences of dishonesty. Robert, who celebrated his 21st birthday only five days before being convicted in July of obtaining property by deception and handling stolen goods, appeared in court on two subsequent occasions for sentence but the pre-sentence reports were not completed and he was further remanded on bail.

'On Monday, the welfare report was ready but solicitor Jeff Bannister told magistrates sitting in Wells that his client had died. Court Chairman Roy Hewett said, "We are extremely sorry to hear about this." The sudden death has been reported to the coroner.'

I found Liz Barton in the cluttered office the *Big Issue* shares with the fledgling Robert Barton Trust, a charity she and friends set up to aid and advise the lost and homeless of Glastonbury. On her desk and on a side table rested identical photographs of a youngster – plainly her late son. In the pictures Robert bends over sideways, a puzzled smile on his face. His arm is flung out and his thumb jerks up, as though he is hitch-hiking.

His boyish, untroubled face, his jokey, artless pose for the benefit of the photographer and his chums on a bench, makes Robert seem naïve and younger than his doomed 21 years. "It was taken a few weeks before he died," said Liz, watching me study the photograph. "It's the last picture we have of him."

Liz Barton herself was dressed like a traveller: loose shawl, silver ring through a nostril, gold ring round a thumb, beads and a five-pointed star at her throat. Her dark, coppery hair dropped straight as a waterfall to her shoulders. As she spoke of Robert, she was by turns buoyant and weighed down by grief.

"In 1995, we came here from Newcastle as a family, my husband Jim, and Robert and his two younger sisters and I," she began, speaking in a Geordie lilt. "We were sick of life in the north-east. Robert's father and his uncles and both his grandfathers, all of them had worked 9-to-5 factory jobs, or on construction sites. We wanted to break the pattern. We were looking for something more meaningful in life."

Traveller-friends had started a workshop in Cornwall. Did Jim, a furniture upholsterer, fancy coming down? The Bartons seized the opportunity. It was summer. The time was right. They had nothing to lose: the girls were barely into their teens and Robert, at 19, had few prospects at home. He'd left school at 15, done a turn at construction under the YTS and was now on the dole. Jim and Liz bought a 12-foot caravan and, after bidding goodbye to Liz's elderly parents, the family headed south. "Leaving his grandmum was hard on Robert," Liz added in an odd tone of foreboding.

"We were in no hurry," she went on. "It was brilliant to have the freedom to pick and choose where we wanted to go. Brilliant. We built campfires. We cooked under the stars. We slept in the caravan. It was all new and exciting for the kids." Coming along the ridge of the Polden Hills from the M5, the family glimpsed Glastonbury Tor. Robert was dumbstruck, as though the Tor beckoned him towards some New Jerusalem. All he could say was, "Wow, Mum, look at that hill".

They pitched camp in a drove near Snow's Timber Yard at the bottom of Glastonbury and next day, midsummer solstice, they made their first ascent of the Tor. The hill was alive with celebrants: jugglers, drummers, card readers, tellers of Glastonbury fables. "Robert disappeared, and we didn't see him again until the next morning," Liz recalled. "He said he'd had the time of his life – all that talk about mysticism and folk stories, and about the tunnel leading into the Underworld. From then on, he went up the Tor every single day. Every, Single, Day. Sometimes he would spend the nights up there, just listening to music and sitting round talking."

Glastonbury was magic; all previous dreams of Cornwall were forgotten by the Bartons. All the while, they were moving their caravan from site to site; by the autumn of 1995 they were settled in a field on the other side of the Poldens. Under a Mendip housing benefit scheme, Robert then got a flat by himself in the nearby village of Ashcott. He supplemented his dole money by selling the *Big Issue* on the streets of Glastonbury. "He was a terrible salesman," recalled his mother who, as the town's *Big Issue* chief, ought to know. "He'd spend hours talking to people, getting to know them. He'd go into the church to talk with the old ladies."

In January of 1996, only months after he arrived in Glastonbury, Robert's world began to crumble. His grandmother died in Newcastle. He and his mother travelled north by train for the funeral. "When we arrived, Robert wouldn't go to the funeral," Liz recounted. "He couldn't bear to see his grandfather. He couldn't bear to even go into his grandparents' house."

What's more, Robert's Glastonbury girlfriend had left him and, under a new benefit scheme, he'd lost his Ashcott flat. He moved in with friends in rooms on Glastonbury's Church Plot, above the High Street crystal shop and overlooking the church. He began to drink on the benches. "If he was getting into trouble, we wouldn't have known," said his mother. "We often saw him, but we couldn't get through to him. He wouldn't talk to us about his problems."

The summer of '96 wore on and, in moments of sobriety, Robert practised his juggling. On the afternoon of September 21, Liz was walking up Glastonbury's High Street when a voice rang out. "Mum, Mum, look at me!" She looked into the church grounds and there was Robert, wearing the tie-dyed green T-shirt he long ago borrowed from her. His arms jerked wide, as he snapped a string taut. A plastic spool, a Diablo, flew into the air. It hung there, then fell and Robert caught it on the string and grinned as he shifted his feet and kept his eyes on the wobbling spool. "That was the last time I saw Robert alive," said his mother.

That evening, Robert declined to join his friends at a party celebrating the autumn equinox. Later in the night, one of the friends returned from the party to find Robert passed out on the benches. He helped, half-carried, the stricken youngster up the stairs at Church Path and, assuming him drunk, propped him into a chair. The next morning Robert was dead, still dressed in his mother's tie-dyed green T-shirt.

After a moment, I asked Liz how deep Robert's depressions might reach. She shook her head slowly. "He didn't commit suicide. He didn't commit suicide," she whispered, over and over. "He didn't commit suicide. The coroner said he choked on his vomit." She added, moreover, that Robert wasn't addicted to heroin – she knew the eyes of a heroin addict – and yet, a massive amount of methadone was found in his blood. Methadone, she explained, was prescribed to bring on a soft high for addicts coming off heroin and, even by itself, can be dangerous.

Liz also said she didn't know what 'crimes' her son might have committed. But they certainly weren't crimes of violence. "He was a gentle boy," she said. "Just like the vicar said in the church." From her desk she drew a sheet of paper. It had been left amid the flowers at the bench where her son had lain. The sheet of paper bore a black and white reproduction of the Tor, its ruined church tower rising against an empty sky. Under it was a handwritten poem, set down like free verse.

> I spoke to you once
> In the little garden behind
> The Tribunal.
> I was impressed by how
> Good natured, courteous and
> Civil you were.
>
> On Saturday evening,
> I passed you and you lay
> Comatose on the benches
> I looked at you and thought
> You were dying.
>
> I wanted to phone an ambulance
> But I told myself you were just
> Drunk, and that it would be
> Best if I did what everyone
> Was doing and looked
> The other way! I did. A few
> Hours later you died.
>
> Sorry

The message was signed 'Tom'. The surname was illegible.

Liz gazed at the poem. "Robert knew a lot of people in Glastonbury and it could have been anyone who wrote it," she said. "It could have been one of the rednecks, one of those town people who hate the travellers, and was now feeling guilty. I've tried to find the man. I'd like to meet him. I really would. I'd tell him, 'it's all right. It had to happen.' I'm only pleased it happened in Glastonbury."

Liz Barton paused. "You know, this poem helped me realise the enormous amount of love and compassion that can be found in this world." She smoothed out the poem, replaced it in her desk drawer and, grinning, folded her arms on her desk. "You asked me earlier for my Millennium Dream. What will I say? I'll say that I dream that more and more love and compassion will be found in this world over the next thousand years."

One last question: Was Robert buried here or in Newcastle, perhaps beside the remains of his grandmother? "Here," Liz replied. "We had him cremated. We scattered his ashes at the top of the Tor." With that, I left and Liz beckoned a New Age traveller, a young man who had been waiting in the doorway. "Come in," she said, "and sit down."

I stayed that night in a High Street bed-and-breakfast called Hangman's House. The derivation of its name came on a metal plaque in the passage outside its door. The plaque read:

Somerset, 1685. The Pitchfork Rebellion
On this site stood the medieval White Hart Inn

On June 22, 1685, James Scott, Duke of Monmouth, who had previously landed at Lyme Regis, marched from Bridgwater to Glastonbury with his rebel army. They lodged in the two parish churches and camped in the Abbey ruins before continuing to Shepton Mallet next day.

James, Duke of Monmouth, the illegitimate son of Charles II, laid claim to the throne on the death of his father in 1685. James II, who was the younger brother of Charles and succeeded him, was a Catholic. Most of the rebels came from Devon, Dorset and Somerset and, being ill-equipped farmers and farm labourers, carried pitchforks to fight the last battle on English soil.

W. MacDonald Wigfield, in *The Monmouth Rebels 1685*, compiled the fates of some 4,000 of the 5,000-odd men who fought with Monmouth. In the book, 'William Russell' and 'John Rutt' appear as two rebels from West Bradley. But I'd searched through West Bradley's records of 'Births, Christenings, Marriages and Deaths', of which there were hundreds over that period of forty years. But none, alas, was a Russell or a Rutt.

The bridge

When Henry VIII's antiquarian John Leland finished poking round Glastonbury, he took what's now the A39 out of town. Riding west, he came to a bridge over the River Brue. 'The river cum to Glastonburi...' Leland wrote in *History and Antiquities of the Nation*, his 1542 report to his king. 'It cometh to a bridge of Stone of four Arches cummunely called Pontperlus, wher men fable that Arthure cast in his Swerd.'

As if in response to such lofty fanfare, the river today breaks into a trot over pebbles as it reaches the A39, the main road between Glastonbury and Street. Then it glides under the most famous bridge on its route to the sea. Called 'Pontperlus' in Leland's day, the bridge later would carry the names Pontem Periculosam, Pon Perilis, Pontparlous and, as the cast-iron marker beside it now proclaims, 'Pomparles'.

As these words imply, a Roman causeway may once have spanned the marshes at this spot. Such a thought intrigued the late, local historian, Stephen Morland, of the family that owned a sheep-skin factory in Glastonbury. "In 1881, my grandfather dug there, just upstream from the current bridge," Morland once told me. "He found oak timbers which might well have been the remains of a Roman causeway. But he didn't find any artefacts that were conclusively Roman." He, Stephen Morland, had dug on the site in 1922 and found a Roman bowl. "It was *under* the oak timbers and this, obviously, suggests that the first bridge at the site was built *after* the Romans."

In any event, Morland continued, the bridge's celebrity springs from Arthurian legend and the beguiling thought of King Arthur's sword, Excalibur, being lobbed into the lake which then covered much of the Levels. "There's no historical grounding for Excalibur," the debunking Morland concluded. "I should think the Glastonbury monks had something to do with it. They were very capable of making use of Arthurian legend."

Excalibur. The legendary, bejewelled sword – a heavy, £165 Spanish-cast 'reproduction' of which I'd seen on sale in Glastonbury – had long been prominent in English fable: from Sir Thomas Malory's *Le Morte D'Arthur* (1470), the version popular in the monks' and Leland's day; through Alfred Lord Tennyson's *Idylls of the King* (1859); to T.H. White's *The Once and Future King* (1939) which, in the form of the musical *Camelot*, rekindled the public's interest in Arthurian legend.

The fables differ slightly in detail but a common sub-plot contends that Arthur, who alone could draw the sword from a stone (or who was given it without fuss by the Lady of the Lake), thus became the rightful King of England. With Excalibur at his side, Arthur ruled his kingdom justly and, it must be said, with much spilling of blood and guts, both male and female.

Crucial to the legend is the image of Arthur, lying mortally wounded, commanding Sir Bedevere, his Round Table knight, to cast Excalibur to 'yonder water side'. Bedevere, wrote Malory, 'threw the sword as far into water as he might; and there came an arm and a hand above the water and met it, and caught it... and then vanished away the hand with the sword in the water.'

Malory makes no mention of a bridge. And no self-respecting poet would mention one today, for Leland's bridge of 'four Arches' is gone, and with it the aura of legend. Single-spanned, flat, fifty-five feet long, the current bridge was built of reinforced concrete by the Somerset County Council in 1923. It was rebuilt in 1973, this time with steel pilings to withstand the weight of 180-ton lorries pounding along the A39. The upstream parapet is made of stone with a concrete post tantalisingly marked 'G 1705' which, alas, turns out to be only a parish boundary mark. The downstream parapet is made of steel palings.

It was from the downstream side, the 'lake' side of the bridge, that Bedevere would have thrown Excalibur. At least John Cowper Powys thought as much in his classic, *A Glastonbury Romance*, published in 1932. In Powys' novel, the anti-heroic John Crow leans against the parapet and peers sceptically into the trickling water of the Brue. 'John's eyes, roaming in search of anything that might recover the ambiguous romance that hung about the spot, fell eventually upon a dead cat whose distended belly, almost devoid of fur, presented itself, together with two paws and a shapeless head that was one desperate grin of despair, to the mockery of the sunlight.'

Crow experiences a rage of 'bitter sympathy' for the luckless creature and, in a state of shock, distinctly sees 'literally shearing the sun-lit air with a whiteness like milk, like snow, like birch-bark, like maiden's flesh, like chalk... an object, *resembling a sword*, falling into the mud of the river.'

I too peered over the bridge's downstream palings and into the trickling waters of the Brue.* Unlike John Crow, I experienced no such epiphany, no dead cat, no chalky-white sword 'shearing the sun-lit air'. Nor did my eyes fall upon some useful symbol of twentieth-century Glastonbury. A drug-user's syringe, perhaps? An unsinkable McDonald's hamburger carton? No. All I saw in the river current was a red mitten, snagged in a clump of reeds. Its palm was turned up, its fingers twiddling in an ambiguous gesture of farewell.

* In 1962-63 England suffered one of its coldest winters in memory. "We could skate down the Brue the ice was so thick," recalled Joe Morland, a friend who at the time lived on Roman Way. He once took me to a spot near the sluice. "The temperature dropped so quickly one night that a swan got frozen on the surface of the water, about here. The next day we found it, just its feet stuck in the ice and bits of carcass and feathers. A fox must have got it."

Willows

Whenever the Australian cricketers come to England to contest the Ashes, I think of sewage. Let me explain.

From Pons Perilis, if you look westwards across the Somerset Levels, you can see a grove of trees that cover the former sewage works of Street. Years ago, the Street Urban District Council operated it also as a farm. Carrots, withies and mangel-wurzels were grown on the nine acres; so were cricket bat willows, elegant trees looking rather like their first cousin, the poplar. In the shit of the Street sewage-works grew the bats that Australians used to beat England at cricket.

The story, like most stories in Street, begins with a Clark – the shoe dynasty that ruled and still rules the town. In 1904 F.J. Clark, chairman of the Council, suggested that coerulean willows, the fast-growing variety used for cricket bats, might profitably be planted. Duly, that spring, 110 sets were put in along the bays of the sewage farm.

"I was in London at the time," he later recalled, "and my brother, who was buying bats for South Africa, told me that the manufacturers found great difficulty in getting a suitable willow wood, and as we were just then planting various trees in the Sewage Farm, I got him to procure sets of the proper willow trees...."

By 1922 the crop had grown, matured, and was ready for inspection. Bat-makers, convinced that suitable willows could only be grown in East Anglia, were coaxed down to take a look. The trees sold splendidly, £515 for the lot, which reduced the town's rates by 9d that year. Clark was delighted. "I hope we shall plant a lot more," he urged the council's Sewage Farm Committee, "so that in 20 years the parish may again benefit in the same way as we have done."

By the late 1920s, the willow business was doing nicely and Doug Bush, our neighbour, was harvesting them. Bush, now in his 80s, was one of the youngest cutters working for Snow's, the Glastonbury timber merchants, and as such he was given the unenviable job.

"It was very pre-historic over there," he told me one evening when we met again at the *Greyhound*, the pub in Baltonsborough. "We had to work knee-deep in waders, right in the sewage bays, and if you were working in a bay that the supervisor wanted to fill up, well, you had to work fast."

Bush was a cricket fan. He and his friends would bicycle the twenty-four miles to Taunton to see Somerset play. Their hero, their distraction from the grim job back in the bays, was Jack ('Farmer') White, the great Somerset and England slow left-hand bowler. "As we sawed, we wondered if this willow or that willow would make it into a Test match," Bush went on. "When the Aussies came, we used to think of our man, Jack White."

Bush savoured the memory. He broke into Somerset-accented doggerel. There was a piece of poetry they'd recite in the sewage farm, he said, and he recited it, insisting on delivering the lines in all but impenetrable Somerset dialect:

> They mid-be proud of Woodfull, Ponsford, Ryder,
> But we've gout our Jack to gee-em cider.
> For he can play the stiddy game,
> Or hit like flashes,
> And bowl their hottest batters all to ashes.

And on they would saw. The willows were cut into three-feet lengths and Jim Cox, who owned lorries in Street, hauled them round the country. "Hertfordshire, Suffolk, Norfolk," he recalls. "Once I took a load to the Tilbury Docks; they were going by boat to Australia." The loads, however, mostly went to that prime bat-making region, East Anglia. One such bat-maker was Edgar Watts of Bungay, Suffolk, who bought clefts from the Street sewage farm until 1969.

"The wood was very, very strong, and very dark," he recalls. "But the wood – how should I say it – was stained. The willows had grown so fast that they drew the sewage up into the wood. English players didn't want it. They wanted pure white bats. So we sent them down to Australia, to Crockett's, the bat-makers in Melbourne. Australians liked the dark wood we got from Street."

In Sydney, Keith Miller* said he had used Crockett bats as a boy. Neil Harvey said he had used Crockett bats on his first tour of England in 1948. Crockett's, alas, is out of business. But Bob 'Swan' Richards, the entrepreneur who may know more about cricket bats than any man in Australia, said: "Crockett made the best handles I've ever seen on cricket bats, and he always used close wood of this very strong colour. Wonderful bats. Ian Chappell used to use them and, I think, Greg Chappell as well."

* Editor's note: Keith Ross Miller MBE was a famous all-rounder who represented Australia from 1946 to 1957 and formed a much-feared (by English batsmen) fast-bowling partnership with Ray Lindwall. Harvey and the Chappell brothers were famous post-war batsmen who all captained Australia.

The sewage trees now stood as neat as a hairbrush on an acre of land. There were lombardy and aspen poplars, blurry, fanning-out withies and a few Canadian poplars planted in the 1920s as wind-screens for the soft fruits of the farm. But when my friend Doug Bush joined me, we were not able to find the coerulean, the cricket bat willow.

Bush knew his way round. "They should be easy enough to find," he said, wandering down a dry old sewage bed. "They're distinctive. They stand up straighter than a withy. Their branches don't droop. They rise in a cone and their leaves are lovely blue-grey." You cut them in autumn, he added, out of the sap season.

Amused at finding nostalgia in a sewage works, Bush went on to explain that the cricket bat willow is always female. It had something to do with the long, resilient fibre that you don't find in the male tree. "The bat willows were planted in the sewage works partly to soak up the smell," he said, "and partly to hold the banks from falling into the bays."

Bush had cut down scores of these trees in 1948. He bicycled over from Baltonsborough, his heavy two-handed American Raker saw heaving and bellowing across the handle-bars, and met the dreaded foreman, Charlie Pinker, at the farm gate. Pinker was a tyrant. He hounded the birds-nesting town boys off his preserve and made hell for the willow-cutters.

"Everything had to be done his way. It was a very pre-historic effort and Charlie made it worse. It was good, tough wood but we didn't examine it very closely. We just cut the logs off where the knots came and piled them on the horse and cart, forty to fifty trees at a time, thirty clefts to a tree. We used to think: 'Is this worth it?' Bush smiled. He drew breath and, closing his eyes to remember, completed the cricket poem:

But Jack, me zunny,
Dunny please forgit.
We be lookin' on from Zummerset.

He shook his head: he could see it now. His love, his life, was watching White. "Old Jack, he was the backbone of Somerset," he said. He took a step back and started prancing down the soft soil. "He'd lumber up to the wicket with this tall, thin action, and bowl with more or less a lob," he said and lobbed his arm over. "Just a lob but it foxed 'em."

After visiting the sewage works, I returned to the river and carried on westward along the levee bank. Below me, spring had broken out on Hulk Moor. Hawthorn bushes, bordering the ditches, were in white flower. Starlings bubbled in the meadow grasses. In such blissful weather, my mind drifted into nostalgia. Bogus nostalgia. My mind drifted into the game of cricket.

I would have loved cricket as a boy. I pictured myself a wristy spin bowler and now, alone on the levee, I paused. I bent my head in concentration. Chin up, I juggled the ball and let my fingers weave a cat's cradle – all very beguiling, just like India's Bishen Bedi, without the Sikh headdress – and, prancing down the levee path, I floated a left-arm leg-break at some hapless clump of weeds. Most of all, though, I fancied myself a stylish lefthanded batsman, a pre-incarnation of England's David Gower. I rehearsed what would have been my favourite shot: a late cut. Head down, hands leading bat, I twisted my wrists and sent a ball darting between the slips. Well played, dear boy. Well played? Nonsense. I've never played a late cut in my life.

My game was baseball. As an American boy before the war, I actually met the great Babe Ruth. In the summer of about 1938 the Babe played in an exhibition game in Syracuse's Municipal Stadium. While meeting youngsters that day, he'd lifted me up by my armpits. I still remember the feeling of the Babe's hands pinching off my blood supply and my arms tingling with delight.

CRADLEBRIDGE FARM

RIVER BRUE

HULK MOOR RHYNE

HULK MOOR DROVE

SHARPHAM
PARK HOUSE

FORMER
SEWAGE WORKS

Sharpham Park

I continued down the river from the sewage works and in a few minutes, glancing west to the Polden Hills, I could make out a cedar tree on high ground about a mile away. Beneath the flat slabs of its bough were a dull tile roof, a chimney and the grey façade of what was once a fifteenth century hunting lodge. This is Sharpham* Park house, which overlooks the brook, by now the River Brue. It was the birthplace of Henry Fielding, who has claim to be considered the first English novelist, and thus the first of all novelists.

> * The Old English roots of the name – 'scearp' meaning steep and 'ham' meaning grazing ground – are appropriate enough: through much of the Middle Ages the steeply-sloping forest, trailing down to marshy moors, was alive with stag, deer and wild pig.

The origins of the park are as hazy as the face it presents across the moors. 'The earliest references to Sharpham by name which I have to hand,' writes a local historian, Michael McGarvie, 'date from 1260 when there was an inquisition to decide if enclosing Sharpham Wood would be harmful to the King's Forest.' The king was Henry III, the wood a slope of land covering some nine square miles of oak, ash and maple trees. It was decided an enclosure wouldn't be harmful. But, adds McGarvie, 'there was no mention of a house.'

The house was first built as a hunting lodge by Benedictine monks at the end of the fifteenth century. The chronicler of the *Perambulations of the Twelve Hides* in 1503 also recorded the work done, or ordered, by Abbot Richard Bere. 'In this park, Abbot Richard lately built, at his own expense, a very handsome manor-house, with a chapel, hall, parlours, chambers, storehouses, kitchen and other rooms and offices.'

It was the building rather than the park, now greatly shrunken and denuded, which attracted my attention. Pevsner poked round it and found 'an eminently interesting house historically and archaeologically – historically in that it was a residence of the abbots of Glastonbury, probably the house in which the last abbot, Richard Whiting, was arrested, and also in that it was the birthplace of Sir Edward Dyer, the poet*, and of Henry Fielding, the novelist.'

> * Margaret Drabble's 1985 edition of *The Oxford Companion to English Literature* dismissed Dyer's chief claim to fame: 'The most famous poem attributed to him, *My mind to me a kingdom is*, is probably not his work,' she says, suggesting instead that the 16th century lyric was penned by Dyer's contemporary, the 17th Earl of Oxford.

Dyer was a fawning poet whose 'devotion to alchemy did no harm to his position at the Court of Elizabeth', according to his biographer Ralph M. Sargent. He was born in 1543 and spent his boyhood years at Sharpham, sunk in melancholy over the early death of his mother. 'When later he wished to express the tearful state of unrequited love,' Sargent writes in *At the Court of Queen Elizabeth: the Life and Lyrics of Sir Edward Dyer*, his thoughts turned to those desolate Somerset moors, overspread from long, wintry downpours, as he mused:

> Shall I, like meads with winter's rain
> Be turned to tears?

At Oxford, Sargent reports, Dyer's 'excellency in bewailing the perplexities of love were greatly admired.' He later joined the court of Elizabeth I where, together with his friend Philip (later Sir Philip) Sydney, he languished as a poet. His thoughts also turned to alchemy. In fairness, Dyer possibly already knew a bit about the occult art for Edward Kelly, one of the chief English exponents of alchemy of the day, claimed to have found the Philosopher's Stone in the ruins of Glastonbury Abbey.

Sargent tells of the poet being sent in 1588 to Bohemia by Elizabeth I to observe Kelly at work. Dyer returned to England and, dining with the Archbishop of Canterbury, spoke in awe of the event: "If I had not seen it, I should not have believed it. I saw Master Kelly* put of the base metal into a crucible, and after it was set a little upon the fire, and a very small quantity of medicine put in, and stirred with a stick of wood, it came forth in great proportion perfect gold, to the touch, to the hammer, to the test."

---

* Of Kelly, or Kelley, himself little of certainty is known, except that he was one of the great English charlatans of the sixteenth century. Thought to have been born in Worcester in 1555, he had fetched up in Prague, then a hot-bed of alchemy, by 1584. There he was to become known as 'il Zoppo' ('The Cripple'), perhaps due to the fact that his ears had been chopped off as punishment for some unrecorded crime or, more likely, due to injuries suffered in leaping from a Bohemian castle. He had been imprisoned in the castle by his erstwhile friend and patron Rudolfus II who, writes Diana Fernando in her exhaustive *Alchemy: An Illustrated A to Z*, 'was crowned, variously King of Rome, Emperor of Bohemia, Austria and Hungary, and Holy Roman Emperor.' Sir Edward Kelly – he had been knighted in better days by Rudolph – died in 1597 or 1598. That he found the Philosopher's Stone in Glastonbury's ruins – or anywhere else, for that matter – is nonsense, of course: such a stone which, according to medieval alchemists, was used to convert base metals into gold, has been sought but never found since before the time of Christ. What Kelly might have found in Glastonbury are notes left by St Dunstan, a tenth century abbot of Glastonbury, who is alleged by some to have been an alchemist, and patron of goldsmiths.

Knighted in 1596, Dyer died without issue in 1607 and Sharpham passed through his nephews before being sold in about 1660 to the Gould family of Somerset. One Gould, Davidage Gould, left a still visible imprint on Sharpham, while Davidage's sister, Sarah, gave birth to one of the giants of English literature. Henry Fielding, whose father Lieutenant Edmund Fielding had been a hero of the 1704 Battle of Blenheim, was born on April 22, 1707 at Sharpham and lived his early years there.

The house and its grounds would appear, romantically distorted, in Fielding's masterwork, *The History of Tom Jones*. 'The Gothic style of building could produce nothing nobler than Mr Allworthy's house,' wrote Fielding of Tom's foster-father's manor house. 'There was an air of grandeur in it that struck you with awe, and rivalled the beauties of the best Grecian architecture....' Views from Fielding's semi-fictional house included one of the distant 'towers of an old ruined abbey grown over with ivy' – namely, Glastonbury, two miles away.

Since then Sharpham has been the residence of a Victorian geologist named Thomas Hawkins, whose collection of Somerset fossils is now in the British Museum. In our time it has been owned by Charles Chenevix Trench, an authority on the nearby Battle of Sedgemoor; and by a friend of mine, Bobby Wallace, advertising director of the Clark Shoe Company in Street. Wallace sold the place after five years because he, like Chenevix Trench, felt it was haunted.

Sharpham's owner now is a women's fashion-wear tycoon, Roger Saul, who set up the Mulberry empire. "We recognise that Henry Fielding was born here which, of course, is fascinating," he told me over the telephone, making no allusions to ghosts. "But we're more interested in the early history of the house. It's been greatly mucked about and we're trying to bring it back to its former glory. Come over. I'll show you round."

Getting to Sharpham Park across the moors was half the fun. The maze of ditches is baffling, as Tom Jones found in the novel. I dropped down off the river levee and struck out along Hulk Moor Drove, a stony cart path that stands above the wetland. It was spring. Out on the flat surrounding fields, hawthorn bushes were in white flower, marking the ditches, and Friesian cattle slumped in the sun. Swallows bounced about on a soft breeze. A mallard clattered up from the ditch beside my feet.

I know that ditch. I was once walking down the path beside it with my Jack Russell when the dog discovered a Welsh cob in the water. The pony, deeply mired in mud, wore a resigned look. She had given up the struggle. We fetched the owner, a local horse-dealer named Tom King, who brought his tractor and a specially-looped rope for the job. He recognised the pony. She'd been in the ditch before. She was 'Lady', a 25 year-old mare he had bought years ago for his daughter in the Exeter market.

"Nobody knows what I give for her," said King, a dark, blunt-fingered little man who is thought by some to have gipsy blood. "And nobody ever will."

He slung his special noose over Lady's neck, started up his tractor and inched ahead. The loop tightened down, but only as far as a restraining knot in the rope. The pony, it was clear, would not be strangled. Then with a clash of gears and a sucking of mud, he hauled her sideways rather than forwards, eyes bulging, out of the ditch.

"I know the way of it," he said, watching the pony, lathered in black slime, clamber to her feet. "I'm 69 years of age and I've been round horses since I were eight, and I never had to call the Fire Brigade in my life." He took the rope from her neck. "Years ago people used to pull horses out of ditches front legs first. My father done it once and the horse laid about for six months and we had to shoot it."

There was no evidence of Lady, or any other pony, the day I walked towards Sharpham Park across the moor. Hulk is not a big moor. It spreads north about 200 acres from the sewage works. On the Ordnance Survey map it is almost totally empty of the symbols shown on the legend. A maroon contour line, representing an indistinguishable ridge running five metres above sea level, wanders like a thread across it. The black lines that denote its other notable features, however, are straight and ordered. They betray the hand of man, of the Glastonbury monks who first drained the swamps: field boundaries, drains, paths, the drove, a single small farm and Hulk Moor rhyne.

I reached a deep cross-ditch, over which stretched a field of buttercups, turned north and, keeping my bearings on the park now gone from view, crossed a field and a footbridge over a rhyne. It was spongy but comfortable going and, for the moment happily disorientated, I wandered into the farmyard of what is marked on the Ordnance Survey map as Cradlebridge Farm.

The farm-owner swung down from his tractor. A friendly dairy farmer, he introduced himself as Henry Tinney. His family had lived for three generations on "How-kmoor."

"How-kmoor?"

"That's how we pronounce it," he said, laughing, "but don't ask me why."

Over mugs of tea in the yard it became clear Tinney knew the Sharpham legends. He brought a we're-all-in-it-together attitude to the matter of the monks at Glastonbury Abbey. "They had their hunting lodge up there at Sharpham and another over at Norwood Park, on your side of Glastonbury," he said. "And the story goes that when they got up in the morning, depending on which way the wind was blowing, they'd go east or west for a day's sport. It's interesting that there is a field over there, just the other side of the lane, called Old Hunt Close."

The sport would have been hunting deer and wild pig in Sharpham Park and, to a lesser extent, fowling in the swamps upon which Tinney's farm now rests. Tinney gave no credence to the legend, widely believed among locals, that the monks had dug an escape tunnel under the moors from Glastonbury Abbey to the outlying safety of Sharpham.

"That's a fairy story," said Tinney. "It would have passed under my pastures and right now we're sitting over seventeen feet of peat – pure peat – and below that it's water-logged blue clay and below *that* it's bits of soap stone. In fact, we once sunk a bore-hole in that bit of pasture. We went down one hundred feet before we hit anything solid." He stirred his tea with a stick. "You can't tell me the monks could have dug a foot tunnel through peat."

Tinney gave a great, wheezy laugh at such an unlikely feat of engineering. No, he didn't mind my carrying on across his land. "Stay on this side of the rhyne, though, and go through the gate on the left," he said, pointing in the distance. "See the sheep? On the peat works. That's the beginning of Sharpham Park."

I met Roger Saul, and his wife Monty, beside their station wagon in their gravel drive. The fading sun softened and picked out shadows in the façade of the limestone house. It also picked out a pair of numbers and initials punched through the iron of a weather-vane on a wing of the building. They read '1733' and 'D G'.

"The initials stand for Davidage Gould. I believe he was Henry Fielding's uncle – his mother's brother – who once owned the house," said Saul. "The date must represent some building project, maybe the wing. There is a '1701' over on one of the stables. The Goulds were always building or tearing down." He shrugged and led the way to the front door.

Pevsner noted this front door with 'its elaborate iron work, a type familiar in churches but rare in houses.' Saul said he understood that Pevsner had taken only a cursory look at the house but he agreed that the front door probably was a former church door. "My guess is that it came out of the abbey," he said and, with a click and a wonderful clank of its iron latch, we stepped into the front hall of the manor.

It smelled of stone. In front of us rose a staircase, dark oak, with heavy balustrades which suggested the complex problems which Saul faced in sorting out the history of his house. A finer staircase of the house, dated 1726, and presumably the main staircase, now resides in the Victoria and Albert Museum in London.

In 1977 the Wallaces bought the house from Chenevix Trench, then a master at nearby Millfield School. Mrs Chenevix Trench took Christine Wallace aside. "I have to warn you, my dear," she said. "There is a presence in this house. A sound of walking. And a weird sweet smell, rather like burning incense, at the top of the staircase in the hall."

The staircase smell was to worry the hard-sniffing family dog, but not its master. Bobby Wallace is a practical, robust, no-nonsense sort of Scot by nature. "I never believed in ghosts – that is, until we lived in Sharpham," he told me years later, after his wife had insisted they move from Sharpham to a nearby farmhouse. "When we bought Sharpham," added Christine, "we bought a ghost."

Their worst haunting didn't take place on the sweet-smelling staircase. It took place in the first floor Harlequin Chamber, Fielding's nursery. This room, I later read in Wilbur L. Cross's biography, *The History of Henry Fielding*, 'is finished in oak panels, with many cupboards, one of which opens into a dark hole known as the ghost's room.'

Oak panels and cupboards still furnished the Harlequin Chamber when the Wallaces used it as their master bedroom. "For years we slept there soundly, with the head of our bed pushed against the oak panels. Until one morning, at about four o'clock, this noise came from behind the panels," Bobby said. "It was a loud dragging noise – no chains, not that kind of thing – just a horrible noise, like lots of stone or heavy weights being moved."

Christine took up the story. "I wondered if, somehow, it was the children in a far wing of the house. Those were the days when children wore those sort of sleeping bags with big, draggy feet. So I went in to check them. They were fast asleep." The noise continued for about twenty minutes. By then, Wallace had concluded that the sound might be shifting chimney stones, or plaster settling behind the panels. He decided to investigate the following morning and fell back into a fitful sleep.

"The next day I got a jemmy and gently prised away a panel, expecting to find an empty space, or maybe a cupboard," he said. "But no, it was solid. No bits of chimney. No fallen plaster. No nothing. Just solid stone." Wallace laughed, a mirthless croak. "I've had chilling experiences in my life – I was stationed in Malaya in the army – but this was the most chilling I've ever had." I told them that even in Fielding's day, according to his biographer, there was a dark hole back there called 'the ghost's room'. The Wallaces only nodded.

Their chillings didn't stop with the Harlequin Chamber Bump in the Night. There also was the Abbot Whiting Incident. "We had some guests one weekend from London, a public relations man and his girl-friend," Wallace went on. "Very sophisticated people, not at all religious. We put them in Whiting's bedroom, and in the middle of the night the girl woke up to find her man sitting bolt-upright, reciting the Lord's Prayer. Very loudly. He was scared out of his wits. He thought there was a 'presence' in the room."

And what about that smell at the top of the stairs? Wallace had turned knowingly to his wife. It was this smell, or at least *a* smell, they agreed at the time, that brought on Christine's collapsed lung, which finally drove the Wallaces from Sharpham. "It turned out that where I had been teaching a school music class in a pottery room, there was a faulty kiln. It emitted sulphur and I'm allergic to anything sulphuric," she said. "But at the time we thought my collapsed lung was caused by the smell at the top of the stairs. We moved from Sharpham a year later."

Meare and Westhay

Cradled in ancient man-made levees, the waterway travels sluggishly through the hamlets of Meare and Westhay, past the village cricket field at Bason Bridge before suddenly, as if smelling the sea, it picks up pace and flows under the M5 motorway.

In living memory, Meare was so flood-threatened that people kept row-boats in their back gardens, a measure that enhances the villagers' sense of embattlement and pride. That and the cruelly disproportionate loss of something like two dozen sons in World War II. An old lady, now dead, talked to me about these men, peat-diggers "stepping over the hedges and going to war." One November 11, I heard the vicar speak beside the war memorial, one of the thousands of memorials and cemeteries throughout the nation.

Meare's most famous resident, a retired peat-digger named Ray Sweet, uncovered the timbered 'Sweet's Track', which is carbon-dated back to 3800 B.C. and said to be the oldest road in Europe, possibly the world. Sweet's name is known throughout the archaeological world but, for him, memories are of fist-fights between the boys of Meare and Westhay.

I walk on, picking up the Brue as it trundles out of Meare toward Westhay. Off to the north, and over the drained Iron Age Meare Pool, I make out the grey limestone cliffs of Cheddar Gorge. This vast, intricate cave, with an underground river, was, according to one school of thought, the inspiration for one of English literature's most haunting scene-setters: 'caverns measureless to man.'

The sky is big and empty near Westhay. Picked out against it, a figure came down the drove in a slow, swirling limp. As it drew nearer, I made out an old woman, walking with the aid of a stick. She looked frail and in danger of stumbling, and when she got close I asked her where she was going. She clamped her stick against her hip to steady herself and, with a broken-tooth grin, indicated a nearby cottage. "That is my house," she said.

Immediately she spoke, it was clear: she was Italian. Also, that accent suggested the likely path of her life. She must have some connection with the many Italian Prisoners of War who had stayed on, after working on a local farm during the conflict. There are many such Somerset Italians: farmers, builders, stone-masons, shop-keepers.

Later, over tea in her kitchen, I heard about Angelina Ponsillo. Her late husband, Dominico, had been a PoW and a wartime farmhand in Somerset.

Signora Ponsillo had lived in this country half a century but her English was poor and now, rising 80, her memory poorer still; in consequence, her son Rafael, born in Somerset, came in from the farmyard to translate and fill in the gaps of her story.

One of ten children, Angelina was born in a village outside the town of Ciazzo, in the mountains north-east of Naples. Both her family and Dominico's had been tenant farmers, sharing their crops with their land-owners. They grew most of their food: pigs, a cow, maize, olives, fruit, she said. They netted blackbirds and swallows to cook and put on their pasta. Life was hard, and yet the signora recollected the smells of grapes in the vineyards and peach blossoms in the orchards. She remembered the sounds of grillos ("crickets," according to Rafael) throbbing through the hot summer nights.

If hard, her life also was religious. She and her sisters once made a pilgrimage to the shrine at Monte Virgine. How far away was that? "Far, far," she replied, with a flap of the back of her hand. Rafael knew: he'd been to Monte Virgine. He said it was ten miles from her village, more or less. His mother then broke into a thicket of Italian. He heard her out before explaining: she was talking about her village church. It was surrounded by a thick stone wall in which there were vaults to receive the coffins of the dead. "Mother's parents are buried in that wall," he said. "In Italy, or at least in the poorer parts of Italy, there is a feeling that only poor people are buried in the ground." In an aside to me, he added: "for years, Italians over here hated the thought of being buried in the ground."

She heard him. "I want to be buried beside my husband in Glastonbury," she insisted in English. "Yes, Mother," replied Rafael. "But now we must talk about the war." When the war came, Dominico went. He was her promesso sposo, her betrothed, and the two wrote regular letters. In 1941, his letters suddenly stopped. He'd been captured in North Africa. "He lay on his stomach in the hot sand – being strafed by Allied airplanes. Running, then lying in the sand, Father said it was the worst two days of his life. He prayed the planes, flying low and shooting at him, were American. American pilots had bad aim." Rafael smiled at me in good humour; plainly he had recognised my accent.

Meanwhile, in Italy, the war raged on. The signora nodded as her son told how she and her sister had stumbled through the fields to escape being raped by German soldiers. She listened as he told how her family had lived nightly 'under the ground' in a dug-out, covered in brush and turf, and how the Allied bombers flattened the nearby monastery of Monte Cassino.

Then, one day, Dominico's father burst across the olive groves with the news: his son was safe, he shouted, waving a message. Safe in an English war camp. Dominico and Angelina resumed their correspondence and in

1948, after the fighting, he returned home. They married in the church surrounded by the walls of the dead. He brought her to Somerset where a job awaited him on the same farm he'd worked on during the war.

Dominico was a hard worker, and gregarious. He integrated. "He was always volunteering to help the neighbours," Rafael recalled. "And the English treated him well." So well, in fact, that in 1954 he was offered the Burtle farmhouse where we sat, with twenty surrounding acres, all at a generously low price.

The conditions, under regulation, were simple but inflexible: four years on a farm. He urged friends and relatives from Ciazzo, dirt-poor farmers, to take up the offer and start new lives in Somerset. No fewer than five heads of family did so, some eagerly, some with reluctance. "Dad claimed he didn't really want to come," recalls an amused son of one of these settlers. "He only came to keep Dominico company."

The Five Tribes of Ciazzo, if that is the term, were joined in this area of Somerset after the war by former PoWs from other parts of Italy. Few, if any, became British citizens, clinging as they did to the dream of one day returning home. Dominico longed to return to Ciazzo one day, to farm, and when he died to be interred in a stone wall. His farm on Green Drove, which leads to the River Brue, became a hub of expatriate Italian social life, of wine-making and salami.

The names told a tale of assimilation. As we sat in the kitchen, Rafael was joined by his son. Rafael was born in Somerset but named after Angelina's father in Italy. Rafael's son was also born in Somerset, but named Nathan, after Diana Ross's pop song, *Nathan Jones*.

The old lady once had hoped to spend her last days with her husband in Ciazzo, where the spring air is scented with peach blossoms, to the sound of crickets, and perhaps to finally rest in a vault in a church wall. "But I am too old now," she said, and besides, her husband was gone. She will be buried beside him in a Glastonbury cemetery.

I leave her and, on another day, I visited the Italian Corner – the northwestern corner – of Glastonbury cemetery. There lies 'Dominico Ponsillo, died June 5, 1994, aged 77 years' with an oval photograph. In a cap and plaid work shirt, with an infectious grin, he looked like a happy lumberjack.

On a few obviously English headstones were oval, glass-cased, colour photographs of the deceased. This, the local funeral director would tell me, was an increasingly popular custom borrowed from Italians resting in the cemetery. And beside Dominico, a little lower on the slope, an empty space for his wife, Angelina Pasquela.

Fatal affray at Mark

"There was an inn called the *Black Bull Inn* and a road ran past the front door," said the prosecuting attorney, Mr Douglas Metcalfe, opening the manslaughter trial at the Taunton assize in January 1899. "If people turned to the right they went to a place called Mark. But if they turned to the left they went down a road and got to the River Brue, across which there was a bridge."

The bridge still stands. Beside it, just over its hump, is a tiny cottage which for years bore a simple wooden plaque which read:

In memory of Albert E. Watts
Who was Killed on this Bridge, Nov. 18, 1898
Aged 33 Years
Left a Wife and 5 Children

The plaque, with its story, has been embedded in local lore for a century. "As a boy, I used to see the plaque when I was sent over the bridge to get cider at the inn," a local farmer, then aged 90, once explained to me. "I must have been about seven at the time because I was learning to read. I was learning to write too, and I remember cutting my initials, 'R.N.' – like Royal Navy – on a stone halfway across the bridge."

Ronald Norris paused to smile, pleased with his 'R.N.' word-play, before turning his mind to the violent death of Albert E. Watts. "The way I do understand it," he said, "this chappie Watts, he be hit on the head with a bottle. Then he be chucked into the river and drowned."

The old man's memory was imperfect. Indeed, many local memories of the incident are imperfect for, according to contemporary *Bridgwater Mercury* newspaper accounts of the 'Fatal Affray at Mark', Watts did not drown. He died on the floor of his cottage. A post mortem examination, moreover, found a large clot of blood on the brain which corresponded to a bruise on the back of the head. The head injury, concluded the district coroner, 'was undoubtedly the cause of death.'

Testimony at the coroner's inquest, the magisterial proceedings and the trial at Taunton, all copiously covered in the *Mercury*, told a brutal story.

On that November night, a farmer named Frederick Larder, 26, treated the labourer Watts to a drink at the *Black Bull Inn*. "They did not drink out of the same cup, as one was drinking half-and-half and the other a pint of cider," recalled the landlord, Mr Isaac Tratt. The landlord's son, Henry, would add that the men appeared sober when they left the inn at about nine o'clock and began walking towards the bridge.

As they approached the bridge, Watts' eight-year-old son stood in the cottage door, holding a lantern to guide his father in the dark. The boy,

Henry, would testify that Larder suddenly shouted at his father: "You stabbed my horse!" By lantern-light, the boy saw Larder strike his father down. Young Henry threw stones at Larder. The boy's mother rushed out of the cottage. "What hast thee done to my husband?" she cried, according to the *Bridgwater Mercury*. "Nothing," Larder said and, turning, walked away. "Thee hast!" she shouted after him. "And I'll make thee know better tomorrow."

The boy ran for help to the inn. When the landlord and his son reached the scene, they saw Larder's father, mother and sister standing by the bridge, "rendering the stricken man no assistance." Watts was laid unconscious on his cottage floor but his wife didn't send for a doctor until the following morning. "I didn't think he was that far gone," she said later. By the time she went to the expense of calling a doctor, Watts was dead.

Also that morning Larder went to the *Black Bull Inn* to have a word with the landlord's son. In their conversation, according to the young Henry Tratt, Larder said: "What have I done so bad that people say I did last night?" To this young Tratt replied, "I should think it was a shame to knock a man down like that, as the little boy said you did, and leave him on the road like that."

"I have never hurt you, Henry, have I?" said Larder. Tratt responded: "No, I don't know that you have. Or done me any good." Larder then told the court that when he left the inn he had gone home directly across the fields. "I don't think you did," corrected Tratt. "I saw you go up the road along with Albert."

Then, allegedly, Larder made a suggestion of which the prosecution would make great play. "I could do you good," Larder told Tratt. "I could lend you £5 now, if you want it." Tratt was above the bribe. "I don't want it, Fred," he said.

If this was a bribery attempt, it was a hefty one. In 1898 five pounds was good money, equal to £178 when, ninety years later, I first read accounts of the trial. The magisterial proceedings had been at nearby Axbridge. The trial was at Taunton, the county seat, and was heard by Circuit Court Judge Sir William Grantham in January 1899.

Sir William, according to *The Concise Dictionary of National Biography*, was a Sussex man and a former Conservative Member of Parliament, an 'industrious, energetic but garrulous judge… a model gentleman and good judge of horses.' More revealingly, as *The Times* would point out at the time of his death a dozen years later, 'the learned Judge a little too often backed his own opinion against the evidence.'

Grantham had travelled by rail from Dorchester to Taunton to preside over the session and, as befits such a dignitary, was received at the railway station by Somerset's high sheriff and the sheriff's chaplain. His lordship, escorted by a posse of the county constabulary, was driven up the High Street in the sheriff's carriage and past Taunton Castle where, more than two centuries earlier, Judge Jeffreys had conducted an episode of his Bloody Assizes. The carriage rattled on to the circuit court judge's lodgings at the Shirehall with the bells of St Mary's ringing a peal of welcome.

At the time, Taunton (population: 20,000) was little more than a market town and its citizens were thrilled by an appearance of an Assizes judge. They were proud of their Shirehall, a massive, stone, 40 year-old Tudor-Gothic building with two vast, peaked courtrooms. Its stately vestibule was made all the more stately by marble floors and marble busts of such Somerset worthies as Henry Fielding, 'Father of the English Novel'; John Hanning Speke (1827-1864), discoverer of the source of the Nile; and John Locke (1632-1704), the philosopher 'who dared to scan the unexplored recesses of the mind.'

Beneath the Shirehall lay another recess, scarcely less explored: an underground tunnel, a quarter-mile long, linking the hall to the city jail where, in living memory, as many as 7,000 sightseers would turn up to witness a public hanging.

The jury consisted of a dozen men chosen from a panel of twenty, all landowners and including five Colonels and a Captain. His Lordship congratulated them on the fact that Somerset was 'free from any serious crime.' Save one, he said, no case 'of any great importance or unusual difficulty would be presented to them.'

With that, Sir William got down to the business of dispensing justice. He worked with self-assurance, and swiftly, for in two days he would hear eleven cases. Seven of these would result in conviction by the jury and sentences of hard labour from the bench. A pair of Bridgwater poachers, for instance, each got three months for 'being on land for the purpose of taking game.' A Yeovil bigamist received nine months for leaving his wife and six children before marrying another woman (and then leaving her). A Bath coachman, convicted of drunkenly assaulting his employer with a stable broom, faced a year of hard labour. A labourer 'weak in intellect but a good workman' got four months for a crime so unmentionable the press didn't mention it.

By 11.30 a.m. on the third day of the session only one case, the twelfth, remained on the criminal calendar. This was the one that Grantham had told the jury would be 'very unusual'. This was the one in which Frederick Larder, 26, farmer, was charged with 'feloniously killing' Albert Edward Watts, farm labourer, on Mark bridge on the night of 18 November, 1898.

Judge Grantham's crowded courtroom was hot and stuffy that day. Scarcely had the prosecuting attorney set the scene of the crime in his opening remarks when, as the *Mercury* reported, 'the proceedings of the court were interrupted by the fainting of an elderly gentleman who was occupying a seat in the jury box. He was removed by several policemen. His Lordship directed that the windows be opened.'

Not long afterwards came a moment of levity when, amid laughter round the courtroom, the judge implored Police Constable Perry to cease using the word 'diseased' in reference to the dead man. "Please say 'deceased'," instructed Sir William.

The alleged bribery attempt cut no ice with the judge. Nor did the coroner's report that Watts' inner lip was cut, a wound consistent with a blow from a fist. Nor, for that matter, was there corroboration that Watts had stabbed Larder's horse which, in Larder's defence, might presumably have been entered as due provocation for the assault.

Six hours of evidence was heard in court and, afterwards, the judge expressed the opinion that the evidence was not sufficiently complete to warrant the jury finding a verdict of guilty. 'After an absence of half-an-hour,' concluded the *Bridgwater Mercury* report, 'the jury returned into Court with a verdict of not guilty. The prisoner was discharged. His Lordship rose at 6.15.'

As I prepared to continue down the river, an image remained vivid in my mind: little Henry, the eight-year-old Watts boy, a lantern swinging in his hand, gazing down on the fallen figure of his father on the bridge. Whatever happened to the boy? And to his four siblings? And to Watts' wife who sat with her unconscious husband for half a day before seeking a doctor?

There are no fewer than 186 Wattses in the local telephone directory – it's a common Somerset name – and I've spoken with a dozen who live near Black Bull Bridge. None can – or will – shed light on the fate of Albert E. Watts' family. One namesake said, "they've gone without trace." So, it seems, have the Larders. The one Tratt in the area denies any link with the *Black Bull Inn*. In fact, there is no more *Black Bull Inn*; it's been a private farmhouse since after the First World War.

As for the plaque on Watts' now-remodelled cottage, which I like to think was raised by Watts' widow as both a memorial to the man and a protest against the judgment, it's gone. It was stolen in 1988. What's more, the old fellow in the carpet slippers, 'R.N.', and his initials, are gone – he under a gravestone in the nearby Burtle village churchyard, while his initials have dissolved under the lichen that now covers Black Bull Bridge.

IN
MEMORY OF
ALBERT E WATTS
WHO WAS KILLED
ON THIS BRIDGE
Nov 18th 1998. Aged 33 yrs
LEFT A WIFE & 5 CHILDREN

Angie's pillbox

In the Second World War, when Britain was threatened with invasion by the German armies, a chain of 'pillboxes' were erected from the Bristol to the English Channels. Along the Brue, from Westhay to Highbridge, there are twenty-six such mini-forts, all octagonal, all with brick walls three-feet thick. These war relics now are crumbling away, too damp for farm storage, their walls sprouting coarse grass and occasionally wild roses.

Back in the Seventies, the pillbox just downstream from Mark Bridge was the hideout of a tiny, red-haired girl called Angie Whitcombe, who grew up in the farmhouse which once was the *Black Bull Inn*. "The moors were a lonely place for a child and sometimes I used to take my cornet and go down to the orchard," she told me years later. "I'd grab a few apples, and climb inside the pillbox."

"The swallows would fly out and if one of their babies fell from the nest, I'd give it a little cuddle and put it back in. Then I'd tip-toe over the puddle of water on the floor and sort of manoeuvre myself up on to one of those ledges to keep dry. I'd practise my cornet for hours. I'd play my scales, or maybe Christmas carols, or hymns, and if it was cold I'd wear gloves with the finger-tips cut out. The pillbox made a lovely noise. You could feel it round you and, I'm told, you could hear it up and down the river for miles. It drove the fishermen crazy."

Angie, still tiny and red-haired, is now Mrs Browning, the mother of three. She lives in a cottage on the river bank, some eight miles from Mark Bridge. "I've still got the cornet, but I don't play it much any more," she said, and laughed. "Only when I want to drive people crazy on their birthdays."

Angie's pillbox now is overgrown. Standing beside it, I paused to look around me. There, on the coast to the north-west, rose the bald Brent Knoll, scene of the great battle against the Saxons in 847. And the defining battle of the Monmouth Rebellion, fought on July 6th, 1685, took place on the King's moor at Sedgemoor, on the other side of the Polden Hills, only about half a dozen miles from the basin of the Brue.

On my map, there appeared a cluster of tiny hillside villages which had contributed men to Monmouth's ill-fated army: Woolavington, Puriton, Catcott, Edington, Chilton Polden. Chilton Polden, especially. The village, according to Wigfield's *The Monmouth Rebels*, contributed thirteen men to the hapless cause: Carver, Dan; Carver, John; Gilling, John; Godfrey, Wm; Hawker, Ric; Keel, Geo; Keel, John … in all, thirteen men from a village which, in the 1991 census, numbered fewer than 600.

Of Monmouth's unlucky thirteen, one was unaccounted for, one pardoned, five reported 'out in the rebellion and at large', one possibly bought his release after sale of his property, two were hanged, another died awaiting transportation to Barbados, and two more perished at sea on the same voyage to the Caribbean.

The royal retribution was terrible and swift. More than 300 rebels were hanged after summary conviction, executed by the autumn of 1685 after the 'Bloody Assize' of the brutal Judge George Jeffreys.

Daniel Defoe

Another rebel – but one who escaped transportation or, for that matter, punishment of any kind – was a young Londoner called Daniel Foe. A young Protestant Dissenter, he saw Somerset with the insurgent army of the Duke of Monmouth. Later, under his chosen name of Daniel Defoe, he became a towering giant of English letters and, for my purposes, an observer of the life and land round what one day would become the town of Highbridge.

Daniel Defoe, according to his rare portraits, wore a diamond ring, a richly laced cravat, sometimes a sword and a wig that bubbled down to his elbows. This prevailing coffee-house image, excessively foppish even in Defoe's day, contrasts sharply with the police-blotter description of the man that appeared in the *London Gazette* of January 1703. 'He is a middle-siz'd* spare man,' read the Man-Wanted appeal, 'about forty years old, of a brown complexion, and dark brown coloured hair, but wears a wig; a hooked nose, a sharp chin, grey eyes, and a large mole near his mouth.'

> * That the authorities should find Defoe unremarkably 'middle-siz'd' may itself seem remarkable to the modern reader. Defoe stood five feet four inches tall, about average for an Englishman born in the mid-seventeenth century.

A tempting reward of £50, worth about £3,500 at the time of this writing, was offered for information leading to Defoe's arrest for 'seditious libel', following the recent publication of his pamphlet, *The Shortest Way with Dissenters*. This work, a stinging satire on the Church of England, greatly displeased the devout Queen Anne and, once convicted, Defoe was sent to London's Newgate Prison. There, he was forced to stand in the public pillory, his neck and wrists clamped in an upright wooden frame. Fruit, vegetables, rotten eggs, even clawing cats were commonly thrown by the multitudes at such prisoners. Defoe, on the other hand, was a hero of the people and is said to have been pelted by flowers.

Upon his release in November, 1703, Defoe returned home to Hackney, East London. Days later, high winds blew tiles from his house and propelled Defoe into perhaps his greatest piece of journalism, *The Storm; or a Collection of the most Remarkable Casualties and Disasters which Happened in the late dreadful Tempest both by Sea and Land*. The 1703 storm, Defoe claimed, took some 8,000 lives, including about 1,500 seamen round the coast and the Bishop of Bath and Wells who was 'found with his Brains dash'd out.'

'As a piece of reporting, *The Storm* is a masterpiece,' wrote Richard West, himself a highly regarded British reporter, in his biography of Defoe, 'which puts to shame all modern accounts of disaster, whether in books, newspapers, radio or television… and fully deserves to be published again, if only for students of journalism.'

In our time, Defoe's storm blew for months through the pages of *Weather*, the journal of the Royal Meteorological Society, following the high winds that slammed across the South of England on October 15-16, 1987. While not rushing to agree with Defoe's view that the 1703 blow was 'the most violent Tempest the World ever saw', the British meteorologist Hubert H. Lamb studied much of Defoe's research before concluding in a special (March 1988) issue of *Weather* that there was 'little doubt that (Defoe's) was a greater storm than the recent one in 1987.' Lamb later joined with a Danish meteorologist to rank storm severities down the ages in their book, *Historic Storms of the North Sea, British Isles and Northwest Europe*. Defoe's came fifth, while the 1987 storm came eighth.

Years later, while collecting material for *A Tour Through the Whole Island of Great Britain*, his three-volume report on the state of the nation, he rides into Somerset. Immediately, his passage is blocked. The diminutive Defoe, nearly sixty years old and barely withers-high to a horse, finds himself 'surrounded with beggars, to such a degree, that we had some difficulty to keep them from under our horse heels.' He plunges on through 'Bridgewater'*, dwelling there long enough to discuss the sad fate of the Duke of Monmouth. Then, moving on, he discovers that the low, rolling coastline is 'not always passable, being subject to floods and inundations, I mean, dangerous to travel through, especially for strangers.'

* Defoe's sentences, tripped up by commas, do seem to run on a bit for the modern eye. But that's the great Defoe and I'll take him rather than leave him. Still, he could have done with a sharp-eyed sub-editor. The town, since medieval times, has been spelled 'Bridgwater', without the middle 'e'.

If you reckon Defoe's ride on the Ordnance Survey Map, you see that he must now be on marshy moorland near where Highbridge will stand in the future. 'All this part of the country, viz. between Bridgewater and the sea, and on northward upon the coast, lies low, and is wholly imployed in breeding and feeding of cattle,' writes Defoe. He goes on to cite the great number of oxen, 'as large, and good, as any in England' that are fattened for the London market on the rich marshy soil; and the 'large Cheddar cheese, the greatest, and best of the kind in England'; and the colts 'bred in great numbers in the moors, and sold into the northern counties, where the horse copers, as they are called in Staffordshire, and Leicestershire, buy them again, and sell them to London for cart horses, and coach horses, the breed being very large.'

Also, and not surprisingly, Defoe returns to a topic close to his reporter's heart, the wrath of nature: 'This low part of the country, between Bridgewater and Bristol, suffered exceedingly in that terrible inundation of the sea, which was occasioned by the violence of the wind in the great storm, anno 1703,' he wrote, 'and the country people have set up marks upon their houses and trees, with this note upon them, "thus high the waters came in the great storm": "thus far the great tide flowed up in the last violent tempest"; and the like.'

Defoe also noted: 'And in one place, they shewed us, where a ship was, by the force of the water, and the rage of the tempest, driven up upon the shore, several hundred yards from the ordinary high water mark, and left in that surprising condition upon dry land.'

Elvers

'In 1337, when the Bishop of Bath and Wells was travelling across Sedgemoor, his party consumed 1,060 eels.' So says the *Natural History of the Somerset Levels* on page 27.

Dave Lewis is a stocky, big-shouldered lorry driver; he hauls animal feed to farms round the south-west of England. He's also a gardener, specialising in tree-lopping, tree-felling, lawn-mowing and patio-building. Lewis's favourite occupation, however, is elver-fishing, and he pursues this passion most nights, on rising tides, between February and the end of April.

"That's when the elvers are running," says Lewis. "They've come a long way. They've come from the Sargasso Sea. And now they're wriggling up into our rivers." He smiles in admiration. "Fabulous creatures."

Indeed, the elver and the eel are the stuff of fable. They have engaged man's imagination down the ages. Aristotle thought they were created spontaneously in the mud, while in the first century Pliny claimed they developed from hair accidentally dropped from the tails of horses. Sir Isaac Walton was lured towards similar hare-brained notions. Eels, he wrote in *The Compleat Angler*, may be bred as 'some kind of bees and wasps are, either of dew, or out of the corruption of the earth.'

A scientific breakthrough came in 1922 when the Danish biologist Johannes Schmidt completed a field study that had taken nearly two decades. Employing Danish research vessels, as well as random merchant ships, Dr Schmidt established that eels came from the Sargasso Sea. The principle elver fishing takes place in the Loire in France and the Severn in England and Wales.

Dave's usual spot on the Brue was shut that night, due to foot-and-mouth precautions, and we go elsewhere. Using a net of his own design, Dave catches only one tray load, but he talks much about the game and later, in the dead of night, we sell his catch to a buyer in a lay-by near Bridgwater. Their destination: Amsterdam, then on to China. It is a profitable pastime, too. On the evening I met Lewis, the slithery, translucent little baby eels were fetching £170 a kilo.

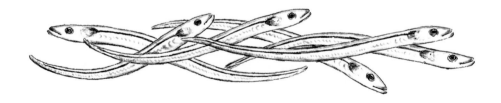

Approaching the sea

Before expiring into the sea, my much-diluted brook reaches the tidal sluice and the mudflats at Highbridge, an unprepossessing town, with a Butlin's holiday camp on one side and the chilling white cubes of the Hinkley Point nuclear power station across the bay.

Coleridge

In August of 1794, Samuel Taylor Coleridge caught his first glimpse of Nether Stowey, a pretty village tucked into a fold in the lower slopes of the Quantock Hills in Somerset. He was travelling on foot with his fellow-poet Robert Southey and Southey's dog, Rover. They had crossed the River Brue at some unrecorded point in walking eighty roundabout miles from Bristol, little more than a stroll for such dedicated ramblers. And now they were approaching what, in a poetical sense, was Coleridge's destination, his well of inspiration. He would return to Stowey in 1797 and there, over the next three years, write three of his best-known poems: *Christabel, Frost at Midnight* and his monumental *The Rime of the Ancient Mariner.*

"Beloved Stowey!" Coleridge would later rhapsodise. And again, when far away in Germany, he'd long for this 'green and silent spot amid the hills'.

Great walkers, the poets also were great talkers, not least the exuberant Coleridge who, his friends said, would become so consumed in expressing himself that his style of walking was affected. In full verbal flow, he 'seemed unable to keep on a strait (sic) line…' the essayist William Hazlitt once remarked, 'shifting from one side of the footpath to the other.'

Coleridge even then was mesmeric, a closely observed super-star, and many years later literary historians, much absorbed in this period of the poet's life, speculate on what he and Southey were discussing as they ambled along the country lane. They might have discussed the plight of Rover, who had come up lame a few miles back or, more likely, the horrific death of their French revolutionary hero, Robespierre, who three weeks earlier had lost his head under the blade of the guillotine. The two poets might well have tried out a few lines of a 600-line verse-drama called *The Fall of Robespierre,* which they would write together over the next fortnight.

Indeed, there was much to discuss. Certainly on their minds was their 'great American affair', their dream of a Utopian commune along the Susquehanna, an Arcadian river in the new American state of Pennsylvania. 'Susquehanna, Susquehanna': Coleridge was enchanted by the very sound of the place and, like a child, he enjoyed feeling the word trip off his tongue.

Coleridge was 21. Son of a vicar of Ottery St Mary, a rural parish in the next-door county of Devon, he'd been sent to Christ's Hospital, a private school in London where, as a sickly child, he was treated with opium, the drug which later would fuel his imagination in another of his masterpieces, the fragmented *Kubla Khan.* At Cambridge he wrote poetry in Latin, Greek and English, drank heroically, travelled to London to visit the whores and, to the displeasure of his tutors, argued the idealism of the Revolution which then was erupting in the streets of Paris.

Approaching his final year at Cambridge, Coleridge dropped out and in a 'mood not far from suicidal', as one biographer put it, enlisted in the 15th Light Dragoons, an equestrian regiment. It was a ludicrous career move for a pacifist and a man who could hardly sit on a horse. After five months, Coleridge was discharged as 'Insane'.

Coleridge was now living in Bristol, struggling to make his way as a poet and literary critic. He had friends there, though, and the past fortnight had been spent walking with Southey, a native Bristolian and like-minded republican. They visited Bath, Wells and the Cheddar Gorge where the caverns, if not 'measureless to man', were sightly enough to be the inspiration for the setting of *Kubla Khan*. They visited a university friend at Huntspill, on the Somerset levels, and another at Shurton Court, a Georgian farmhouse on the slopes of the Quantocks. In Stowey they would meet the wealthy and cultured tanner, Tom Poole, a future friend and benefactor of Coleridge.

The poets and Rover would have approached Stowey – its popular name, then and now – by way of the dirt lane from Shurton Court. This was the route I took more than two centuries later. The lane is now a macadamised road; and, approaching Stowey, it is crossed by the busy A39 bypass, built round the village in 1968. A sign there proclaimed that Nether Stowey is 'twinned with Theillay', a town in the Loire Valley. Would Coleridge have known Theillay? One doubts it. He rarely travelled in France.

As I entered Stowey, however, one thing became clear: Stowey knew Coleridge. There, second house on the right, stood 'Coleridge Cottage'. It bore a plaque: 'Here Samuel Taylor Coleridge Made His Home 1797-1800'. A notice-board added that the cottage, a National Trust property, was open to the public from April to September, on Tuesdays, Wednesdays, Thursdays and Sundays, from 2.00 to 5.00 in the afternoons.

Directly across the street, a pub sign on a mock-Tudor building celebrated what my university textbook back home had called 'perhaps the greatest of all English literary ballads'. The sign, aptly swinging in the wind, read 'The Ancient Mariner'. With a stir of excitement, I gazed at the picture on the sign: it was a banal approximation of the ghostly engraving by the French artist Gustave Dore which appears as the frontispiece to the 1877 edition of the poem. The sign depicted a mariner aloft in a ship's rigging while, above him, an albatross circled round the storm-tossed mast.

However badly the Whitbread brewery artist had rendered Dore's work, the sign's very existence acted as a crooked finger, beckoning the bypasser into the pub. A further enticement was a sticker in the window, boasting

of the pub's entry in *The Good Pub Guide*. I checked my watch. Perfect: before visiting Coleridge's cottage, I'd have time for a bit of lunch, consider what I already knew about Coleridge and Stowey, and perhaps have a word with the publican. He, like the Mariner, might have a tale to tell.

I pushed through the big oak door. Before me stretched a huge pub, with timber beams and horse-brasses and a dining-room off to the side. A blackboard noted the daily specials. Today's were steak-and-kidney pie with chips and peas at £5.95, or Stilton and broccoli tart at £3.95.

In the absence of grilled albatross, I ordered the Stilton and broccoli from the barman. He was a friendly, welcoming man and I remarked that he must do a brisk tourist trade, what with Coleridge's cottage across the street. "In the summer," he laughed, "some people come in and wonder if Coleridge got the idea for his poem from the pub sign."

The pub, he said, was once called 'First and Last', a common name for pubs on the edges of English villages. He pointed to a timber beam on which were hung two framed photographs. Both pictures depicted the local hunt, the Quantock Staghounds, hounds and horsemen, gathered in front of the pub. One, dated 1982, showed the pub sign reading 'First and Last'. The other photograph, dated 1983, was taken under the current sign,

'The Ancient Mariner'. As for the artistic merit of the sign itself, he was not impressed. "The albatross looks more like a seagull to me."

I sat at a table in the pub garden and gazed out over the low, huddling cottages in Lime Street, their roofs mainly red-tiled rather than thatched as they would have been in Coleridge's day. Above these rooftops rose the barren 'Mount', with its out-of-sight Norman castle ruins and, beyond the 'Mount', loomed the distant, green and sheep-strewn Quantock Hills. 'The village itself,' says the Stowey tourist brochure, 'was first referred to in Anglo-Saxon times as being an agricultural settlement on the military road linking royal Saxon estates.'

Flicking fast-forward through history, we see that Stowey's population grew little, if at all, from the sixth century to 1086 when the *Domesday Book* recorded '8 villagers, 9 cattle, 7 pigs and 100 sheep' in the village. Nor was Stowey exactly a boom-town by the 1540s when John Leland, Henry VIII's antiquarian, rode his horse here. 'A poor village,' Leland wrote in his *Itinerary*, 'standing in a Bottom among Hills.'

The 'poor village' nonetheless began to prosper. By 1791, three years before Coleridge's arrival, Stowey was made up of about a hundred houses, mostly cottages, with a rainbow spectrum of 500-odd dwellers: wealthy tanners, such as Coleridge's future friend and patron Tom Poole, candle-makers, clock-makers, cloth-workers, farmhands and quarrymen – the diggers in the lime pits, now disused, that still lie scattered across the hills. In that year, 1791, John Collinson published his massive *History and Antiquities of the County of Somerset*. In it, he describes Stowey as a 'market-town of three streets, built in the form of a Y.'

Stowey still is built in the form of a Y. The stem of the Y is St Mary's Street, running into the village from St Mary's Church, where the ancient mariner begins his tale; the left-hand branch is Castle Street, bounded on one side by a clear-flowing stream, possibly Coleridge's 'dear gutter of Stowey', and on the other by a few fine houses, such as that of Tom Poole; and the right-hand branch of the Y was – and is – the modest, cottage-cramped Lime Street. In Coleridge's day, a cottage called 'Gilbards' stood at the top of the street. It was this 'small, dark, damp and mouse-ridden, cottage', notes the tourist brochure, that Coleridge was to rent from Tom Poole for £7 a year.

Reminders of Coleridge are everywhere in Nether Stowey, but where better to start poking round than at the great man's cottage? When I rang the bell, 'the custodian' Derrick Woolf came to the door. Stocky, bushy-bearded, somewhere in his fifties, Woolf is a shy man, a poetry scholar. He was trained in London as an architect but now publishes poetry collections and a magazine called *PQR*, short for *The Poetry Quarterly Review*.

I told him my mission and, as though any friend of Sam Coleridge's was a friend of his, Woolf welcomed me in. His accent was not West Country. What, I wondered, was a South London boy doing down here? The short answer was that Woolf was devoted to Coleridge, whom he found "an extraordinary character, a spell-binder, a bit like Dylan Thomas." When he heard the National Trust was looking for a Coleridge Cottage 'custodian', he applied and got the job. "In fact, I'm less a 'custodian' and more a tenant," he said. "In exchange for rooms and a kitchen out back, I pay a peppercorn rent and look after the place and show visitors round."

As he went off to make us coffee, I leafed through the Guest Book. 'Interesting'… 'interesting' … the entries went on like this, as if the visitors, seized with embarrassment, found nothing more to say about the cottage. Then, suddenly, a lady from Palo Alto, California, broke the mould. 'The sort of cottage I'd like to live in,' she wrote. Woolf, back with the coffee, smiled at the American's remark. "The lady from Palo Alto might not have liked the mice the Coleridges put up with. The creatures over-ran the place," he said, leading the way into the tiny former kitchen. "But that was Sam's fault. He was too kind-hearted to set traps for them."

The cottage also would have been cold, Woolf went on. The chimney wouldn't draw, and the Coleridges used yards and yards of cloth to stop up the draughts round the windows. Furthermore, the cottage was crowded. Oh dear, was it crowded. Crowded enough for the Coleridge household – Sam, his wife Sara, their infant son Hartley, Hartley's nanny and a young, failing-poet lodger who later would defame Coleridge in a novel. What's more, visitors over-ran the place, rather like the mice. Woolf ticked off these visitors: William Wordsworth and his sister, Dorothy. The essayists Charles Lamb and William Hazlitt. The potter Thomas Wedgwood, who was to be another major Coleridge benefactor. Also popping in was the polymath Humphrey Davy, a Bristol friend who later invented the miner's safety lamp.

"Imagine. Imagine all those people sitting round here," Woolf said, with a wave round the room. Indeed, I imagined half a dozen adults, a squawking infant and the dog Rover, licking a sore paw. I imagined Sara, who hated the place, stumbling over a sprawled-out leg and spilling a pan of boiling milk over Coleridge's foot, as she once so famously did.

The room seemed hardly less cramped now, two hundred years later: Woolf's filled bookshelves surrounded us; the huge wooden table where we sat was piled high with for-sale paperback editions of Coleridge's poetry. There were stacks of postcards picturing the Cottage, and the standard National Portrait Gallery painting of the poet by Peter Vandyke and a modern, suitably surreal illustration of Kubla Khan's 'stately pleasure dome'.

There were also leaflets entitled *Walking with Coleridge in the Quantocks* – three of them for £1 – with commentaries by Woolf and his fellow villager Reggie Watters, editor of the *Coleridge Bulletin*. The leaflets discussed and diagrammed local walks taken by Coleridge and his friends, chiefly the Wordsworths. Illustrated with woodcuts, the leaflets looked enticing and when the front door bell jangled and Woolf broke off to show visitors round the cottage, I had a look.

Leaflet 1, *Stowey*, tells us, among other things, that 'Castle Hill House' on Castle Street was the home of the poet's new Stowey friend, John Cruikshank. 'It was John Cruikshank's dream one night of 'a skeleton ship, with figures in it' that provided the starting point for Coleridge's Rime of the Ancient Mariner.'

Leaflet 2, *Alfoxton*, speaks of the nearby Quantocks mansion which the Wordsworths had leased to be near Coleridge, and the poems they conceived during walks in the area. It quoted Dorothy Wordsworth's view across Bridgwater Bay to the 'Welsh hills capped by a huge range of tumultuous white clouds.'

I was just getting into Leaflet 3, *Kilve* – 'Kilve beach was a favourite spot for Coleridge and the Wordsworths' – when Woolf returned, leaving the new visitors to their own devices. The cottage attracts some 3,000 visitors a year, perhaps two-thirds of them National Trust members on tour of the West Country. Of the other third, perhaps 300 are dedicated, if amateur, Coleridge fans. This number has increased substantially since 1989, Woolf said, when the English writer Richard Holmes published the first of his two best-selling biographies of Coleridge, *Early Visions*, which was followed in 1998 by *Darker Reflections*.

"We also get lots of Japanese visitors," Woolf went on. "They're particularly interested in the Romantic Poets, and have been since Edmund Blunden, the World War One poet, taught in Tokyo in the 1920s. I suppose the metaphysical aspects of Coleridge particularly interest them."

With that, we set out on our tour of the cottage, which amounted to four more pokey rooms, two on each floor, none much bigger than the kitchen. We began on the ground floor. "This was Coleridge's work room," Woolf said, then dropped his voice, as though the poet himself might have been listening from beyond the grave. "He is alleged to have written *Frost at Midnight* here. But I very much doubt it." Woolf's attention then shifted, as every visitor's must, to the full-sized reproduction of the Vandyke portrait of Coleridge. In it the poet, aged 22, is portrayed as full-lipped and soft-faced, podgy it must be said, with innocent, puzzled blue eyes and a luxuriant mane of auburn hair.

"A good likeness, I believe," Woolf said, and went on to quote Coleridge's own assessment of his face. "'Tis a mere carcass of a face," Woolf recited. "Fat, flabby and expressive chiefly of inexpression." He gazed at the portrait, then added: "His mouth's open because he couldn't breathe properly."

"Adenoids," I remarked, getting my oar in. And I, too, found myself entranced by the remarkable portrait. With those facial features, I thought, Coleridge didn't look the durable sort of man who would walk six miles from Stowey to Bridgwater to preach a Sunday sermon at the Unitarian chapel. Then continue on down to Taunton to preach another sermon. Then stroll home to supper over a shoulder of the Quantocks – altogether a 30-mile walk. A pretty tough guy.

We crossed into a second parlour: here were engravings and watercolours of Coleridge and his friends, and a picture of his and Sara's first child, the beloved, vulnerable Hartley, who would die in middle age, brought low like his father by opium.

We climbed a narrow staircase, turned abruptly, and passed down a narrow corridor to what probably was the Coleridges' bedroom. "We now call it the Exhibition Room," said Woolf. On exhibition was a copy of another portrait of Coleridge. This one was done by Washington Allston in 1814, when the poet was 42 and long gone from Stowey. Torn by opium, he looked old now, and even more puffy and perplexed than he did as a youth. There were two untranslated Japanese biographies of the poet in a bookshelf, and drawings inspired by *The Rime of the Ancient Mariner*. In a glass cabinet there were manuscripts and an ink-stand, decorated in the 'Boulle style' and said to have been used by the poet.

I'd begun to share with other cottage visitors a leaden, guilty sense of 'interesting' when Woolf pointed out a ceremonial sword worn by 15th Light Dragoon Silas Tomkyn Comberbache. The sword, its finish gone dull, looked heavy and unwieldy, out of place beside the poet's other memorabilia. Woolf explained. Coleridge, he said, had enlisted in the Dragoons under the alias 'Silas Tomkyn Comberbache'. This absurd nom de guerre was a play on his elder brother's name, Francis Syndercombe Coleridge. Francis Syndercombe Coleridge had committed suicide the year before, while serving in the Indian army.

Near the sword lay a clump of hair set in a gold brooch. This brooch was a curiously poignant object, made all the more so by Woolf's following remark. "Notice," he said. "Sam's hair has gone white. The brooch must have been fashioned late in his life." Had Coleridge's hair gone white with advancing age, I wondered, or had it to do with the opium?

We moved back down the corridor to a bedroom, probably Hartley's, and in Woolf's view probably the room where Coleridge wrote his tender and evocative *Frost at Midnight*. In the poem the infant Hartley sleeps in his cradle while Coleridge, sitting by the low-burning cottage grate, gazes out the window across the snowy, thatched roofs of the village. The poem begins: 'The Frost performs its secret ministry....'

In this silence, broken by the 'owlet's cry', Coleridge meditates on his own childhood and foresees his son wandering 'like a breeze/ by lakes and sandy shores/ beneath the crags of ancient mountains....' In these wanderings, the poet and father feels, Hartley will learn of God through Nature. 'Therefore, all seasons shall be sweet to you.' Then, gazing again through the cottage window, the poet sees 'silent icicles/ Quietly shining to the quiet Moon.'

Scholars have dissected this poem inside out, from top to bottom, from lines 1 to 74, and none more thoroughly than the greatest of all Coleridge-dissectors, the American literary sleuth, John Livingstone Lowes. In his research for *The Road to Xanadu*, first published in 1927, Lowes goes so far as to verify that heavy snow indeed fell in the Quantocks during the 1797-98 winter, the season in which Coleridge wrote *Frost at Midnight*.

As though not to be outdone by Lowe's academic nit-pickery, Woolf added his own speck of knowledge to the mountain of Coleridge scholarship. "I don't think Coleridge wrote *Frost at Midnight* whilst looking through that downstairs window. Couldn't have," he said. "No. I think he wrote it up here in Hartley's bedroom. Because, you see, only up here, under the eaves, could he have seen his 'silent icicles' shining in the moonlight."

Thus ended the lesson on *Frost at Midnight*, and the tour of Coleridge Cottage. However, infected by the craving to do my own matching of place-to-poem, I asked for and got Woolf's permission to stroll down the back garden. Here Coleridge, with all good intentions, had set out 'to raise potatoes and all manner of vegetables' for his family. When his under-attended garden thickened with weeds, however, the poet came up with a charming excuse. 'The weeds you see have taken the liberty to grow,' he wrote to a friend, 'and I thought it unfair to prejudice the soil towards roses and strawberries.'

In the same garden, I soon discovered, Woolf suffered no such compunction. His plot flourished with leeks, potatoes, spinach, Brussels sprouts, strawberries, loganberries, even a struggling apple tree. What interested me more about Coleridge's plot, however, was its proximity to his friend Poole's house and garden. I had a look over its surrounding wall. There was the back of a handsome house, with tall windows and chimneys. But gone was the garden, the arbour, the lime-tree bower, now built-over by sheds.

After Sara Coleridge had spilled the pan of boiling milk on her husband's foot in the crowded kitchen, Coleridge had hobbled his way to Poole's garden, wounded in flesh and spirit and, only months into his marriage, bored with his wife. Crippled by the burn, the poet had missed out on a walk through the Quantocks with the Wordsworths and Charles Lamb. There, under Poole's arbour, Coleridge had composed *This Lime-Tree Bower My Prison*. The poem began with an almost comic and, in the context, endearing moan:

> Well – they are gone: and here I must remain,
> Lam'd by the scathe of fire, lonely and faint,
> This lime-tree bower my prison. They, meantime,
> My friends, whom I may never meet again,
> On springy heath, along the hill-top edge,
> Wander delighted …

'My friends, whom I may never meet again': cut it out, Sam. Was this some sort of parody of self-pity? Was Coleridge, the spell-binder, actually sunk in such anguish? Seeking to solve this sub-textual teaser, I returned to Coleridge's cottage and, thanking Woolf, left him to stalk the shadows of the long-dead poet.

Nether Stowey

The Clock Tower, at the junction of Lime, St Mary's and Castle Streets, marks the village centre. Tall, stone, Victorian – completed in 1897 to commemorate Queen Victoria's Diamond Jubilee – the four-sided tower carried only three clock faces for nearly a century; one pointed along each of the main streets. In the 1990s, however, a fourth clock face was added, giving the time of day to those who had lived for decades in 'Lego-land', the 'new' estate hidden behind the Clock Tower.

'Lego-land', together with post-war housing at the top of the village, has swollen Stowey's population to well over 2,000. Many of these newcomers, these 'imports', are retirees from the south-east of England, many well-paid employees of the nuclear power station at nearby Hinkley Point. Still, or perhaps 'therefore', the village has remained Conservative, dependably doing its bit to keep Bridgwater a safe parliamentary seat. Stowey also is conservative with a lower case 'c'. As one long-time Stoweyite told me: "Socially, it's hard to move in this village. We're not particularly homogeneous. You might say we're divided into non-warring factions."

Outside the Post Office, I met an old-timer called Ken Wilkins, who had been born, bred, and lived most of his life in Lime Street (the name taken from the lime pits, now disused). Wilkins mourned the passing character of the street and the village. There were maybe only six or seven Stoweyites living in Lime Street, he said. And so many newcomers round the village – 'imports' was the village word for them – that he couldn't keep up with the new faces. "I only say 'hello' twice," he explained. "And if they don't answer, that's it."

A signpost pointed a finger to 'Over Stowey', a little hamlet '1¼ miles' higher into the hills. Over Stowey was in the national news during my visit. *The Independent* carried a half-page feature on the 'emotive controversy' stirred up by local plans to 'turn an empty former boarding school into a temporary sanctuary for 72 asylum-seekers from the Balkans, Sudan and Sierra Leone.' The local vicar, an 'import', backed the plan. He had 'enjoyed the benefits of a multicultural population elsewhere' and saw the sanctuary as a benefit to our '100 per cent white population here'.

The locals overwhelmingly opposed the scheme. They cited damages to house prices. They feared asylum-seekers 'chatting up' their girls and, with no money except vouchers, turning to theft. I later met a Stoweyite who had attended a public discussion of the asylum plan. He recalled an Over Stowey lady, worried about walking in the hills with her children, exclaiming: "What if we came upon asylum-seekers speaking a foreign language? The children would be traumatised." He added that he knew of people, older people, in both Stoweys who spoke of the one time they had travelled to London.

The asylum plan was later dropped.

Pausing, I thought now of Parson William Holland, the vicar of Over Stowey in Coleridge's day. The Reverend Holland was a snob, a monarchist, and the bane of Methodists, Unitarians, Catholics and, especially, democrats such as Coleridge and his friends. Listen to the entry in Holland's diary, dated October 23, 1799:

'Went with my wife to Stowey .... Saw that Democratic hoyden Mrs Coleridge who looks so like a frisky girl or something worse that I was not surprised that a Democratic Libertine should choose her for a wife. The husband gone to London suddenly, no one here can tell why. (He was in the Lake District with the Wordsworths.) Met the patron of Democrats, Mr Thos Poole who smiled and chatted a little. He was on his grey mare. Satan himself cannot be more false and hypocritical.'

I walked down the east side of Castle Street and came upon the stream, Coleridge's, dear gutter of Stowey. The poet was a lover of brooks and streams, seeing flowing water as a metaphor for life. It was a fine vehicle for a poem and he schemed one, *The Brook*, while in the Quantocks. He never finished the poem but he got as far as charting its flow. 'I sought for a subject that should give equal room and freedom for description, incident and impassioned reflections on men, nature and society,' he later wrote in *Biographia Literaria*. Imagining this brook, he would trace it 'from its source in the hills... to the hamlet, the villages, the market-town, the manufactories, and the sea-port.'

Today the poet's 'dear gutter' remains a beguiling, clear-running stream, banked and arched in stone, carpeted with pebbles and into which, as a local saying goes, every Stowey boy must fall at least once. Boys also catch trout there, by "tickling their tummies 'til they go dopey. Then you grab them." Here was the stream I'd sought outside Coleridge's cottage and now, to practise my stream-walking, I followed it down Castle Street and, with it, took a right down St Mary's Street.

In *The Buildings of England* Pevsner speaks of 'a few late Georgian and early Victorian houses' in St Mary's Street but he neglects to mention the fire station. The station is less than three miles south of Hinkley Point and of this there is no starker, nor subtler, reminder than a gadget standing behind the training tower. It's called a 'tacki-shade'. Small, open to the breezes, looking rather like an upright butterfly net, it has been put there by the nuclear power authorities to measure dust contamination drifting from the Hinkley Point station.

Stoweyites profess little anxiety over the nuclear plant. They philosophically shrug it off. "We're safe. The prevailing wind blows towards Burnham-on-Sea," says one, while another, more bluntly, suggests: "If Hinkley Point blows up, the whole of England blows up." Ken Wilkins, the Lime Street sage and former Hinkley Point workman, takes a more practical view of the matter. "We've learnt to live with the power plant," he says. "Over the years, it's put food on many a table in Stowey."

The brook gurgled past the fire station, past the playing fields and disappeared under the A39 bypass. Gone, to resurface somewhere on its way to the River Parrett. Across the bypass, marooned from the rest of the village, set beyond a stand of Scotch pines, stood St Mary's church. If the nuclear plant has put food into local bellies over recent years, an established church at this site has nourished local souls since 1311. None of that church remains. What's here now is a church of red sandstone, largely rebuilt in Victorian times, but with a fifteenth century tower topped by a fluttering flag of St George.

Looking sharply both ways, I crossed the bypass and entered the churchyard. On the left of the path, not far from the church's blazing red door, tilted the tomb of Tom Poole (born 1765, died 1837), a bachelor buried beside his parents. Inside, a marble tablet commemorates the achievements of this man 'distinguished for his masculine Intellect', this 'patron of obscure Merit' and friend of the poets Southey and Wordsworth and Coleridge.

Poole took interest in civic matters, not least St Mary's church music, and not long after the Coleridges settled in Stowey in 1797, he appealed to a friend to send 'the Bassoon and the Music' he had promised the church. The bassoon might well have arrived for, three months later, in March of 1798, Coleridge finished *The Rime of the Ancient Mariner*, complete with a 'loud bassoon' sounding in the eighth verse.

There was an organ but no evidence of a bassoon in the church, and when I returned to St Mary's Street, I stopped in at the vicarage. I asked the vicar about the blazing red door. And, er, what about a bassoon? Did he ever get requests for bassoons to be played at a church wedding? The Reverend Phil Denison, a young 'import' from Yorkshire, knew his Coleridge and was amused by the question. He'd only been in the diocese a few years, he said, but no, he'd never had requests for bassoon music.

He raised a finger. However. However, he *did* use various musical instruments during the hymns. In fact, he used a quintet from the St Mary's Worship Team: bass, violin, guitar, flute and piano. "It gets the congregation singing," he said. And with that the Reverend Denison began to sing: "We plough the fields and scatter," his voice rising from a whisper to a jazzy, syncopated rhythm. Then he broke off with a sudden mock-slam of a guitar chord. "Sometimes, I sit in with the group," he said.

And what about the blazing red door? "It's not my doing. It's my inheritance," the vicar replied. "But isn't it a wonderful door? You can see it from miles away in the hills."

On St Mary's Street, a few doors up from the vicarage, stood a large house with a black marble plaque, its gilded letters reading 'The Old House'. This had been Tom Poole's second home in the village. To entice Coleridge back to Stowey in the summer of 1807, to look after his sick friend, Poole had built a bookroom and even a 'sleeping alcove' for Coleridge to escape from his wife.

This was to be my bed-and-breakfast, and I was met at the door by the proprietress, Mrs Marion Gee, an 'import' from the Home Counties. She held a miniature Yorkshire terrier in her arm. Behind them a tiled and lofty hallway stretched to an elegantly-turned staircase. When I told her I was writing about Stowey, she burst out laughing. "You've come to the right place," she said. "If you'd been here in the hallway a while ago, you'd have seen Coleridge stumbling down the staircase." The Old House, she explained, had been used in the film *Pandaemonium*.

The bookroom was my sitting room, and that evening I sat there in the gathering darkness. Coleridge, paranoid, squabbling with his friend, tortured by opium and at the point of breaking up with his wife, had slept alone that summer over there in the alcove. It had been a troubled summer and yet he had managed to write two poems, *Recollections of Love* and *A Dark Sky*. But, at 35, he was almost burnt out. This would be his last visit to Stowey. He would die in London at the age of 61 in 1834.

Richard Holmes, in his two-volume biography of the poet, mentions that a fragment of *A Dark Sky* was composed in the garden below this bookroom. There Coleridge gazes up at the night sky and watches clouds overtake a 'conspiracy of stars'. I crossed to the window. The garden lay in shadow. There was not a star in the sky.

Next morning I returned to Coleridge Cottage and saw Woolf again. One more question. What did he think Coleridge would have made of Hinkley Point?

Sam's cottage curator paused. "He might have liked it. Humphrey Davy was his buddy, you remember, and Davy was a scientist."

Highbridge

"You want to know about Highbridge?" said the woman in the real estate office on Market Street. "You'd better have a word with the undertaker. You'll find his funeral parlour at the end of Springfield Road, under the railway embankment."

I found the funeral parlour at the dead-end of Springfield Road and, fittingly, directly opposite to the town's waste disposal plant. The funeral director responded to my bell ring, and was explaining how and why Highbridge was down-and-on-its-way-out when suddenly his words were blasted away by a long and deafening, two-note whistle cry of a train passing above us.

After the train had passed, and its noise died away, the funeral man said, "They have to blow their whistle at that spot. It's a regulation that's been in force for about two years. Ever since a man walked up on the track and stepped in front of an express train. He was flapping his arms when the train hit him. Mental depressive."

As for himself, the funeral director didn't know Highbridge that well. He'd been there only twenty-three years. Why didn't I see Pat Butt on Coronation Street? He'd keep me talking about Highbridge for hours. I saw Pat Butt. He couldn't talk. He was on his way to a funeral.

Highbridge is that sort of town: depressed – and depressing. In fact, it's rather funereal. It's a cheap-shot target of travel writers. 'Highbridge must rank as one of the least attractive places in Somerset; for thousands it is but a bottleneck incident in their toilsome crawl along (the) A38,' wrote Brian Little in his *Portrait of Somerset*. Little then added: 'It is, however, an interesting though repulsive town.'

The word 'repulsive' struck me as unnecessarily offensive, and 'interesting' as condescending. Yet, he has a point. Highbridge's high street, called Church Street, is a 'bottleneck'. Even after the nearby and parallel M5 motorway was completed in 1972, the long, two-lane, traffic-holiday-bearing Church Street is a headache. Before 1972, it was a legendary nightmare. So clogged was it through the summer holiday season that fable maintains that when Nanny Saunders opened her fish-and-chip shop at 105 Church Street in 1926, she set up on the north-bound side of the road. Why? To cater to hungry Midlander holiday-makers returning home after spending their money in Devon and Cornwall.

"I don't know if that's true or not, but it could be true," Nanny Saunders's grandson, Dennis 'Fishy' Moore, told me in the same shop more than seventy years later. "When I was a boy in the 1950s and '60s, the traffic past here was unbelievable. In the summers, at two o'clock in the morning, it would take you twenty minutes just to get down Church Street – and it's only about a mile long. Even now, people get out of their cars up by the library, walk down, pick up their fish-and-chips and get back in as their cars creep past the shop."

Founder Nanny Saunders ran the shop until 1944; her son George (Fishy's dad) then ran it until 1982, whereupon young Fishy himself put on the white bib and straw hat. What's more, the families lived continuously over the shop. "You get used to the noise and the street fumes," said Fishy. "It's only when you go on holiday that you notice." Fishy takes his family for a fortnight holiday each autumn. This year, for the second time, they're getting away to the island of Mauritius in the Indian Ocean.

If this seems a luxurious break, Fishy deserves it. He works Mondays to Saturdays at lunchtimes, then evenings until 11.30 pm, punishing one-man stints, softened by specialist, thick-rubber shoes "provided for by the catering trade". Into his father's shop name he has inserted the word 'English', so it now reads: 'Moore's English Fish & Chips'. It must be said, nonetheless, that he popped in the word more in jest than jingoism. "A Chinese fellow had just opened a fish-and-chip shop in town," he explained.

Also, Fishy expanded his menu to include curry sauce for the chips, although Asian customers won't eat it; and a top-of-the-market scampi and chips, although neither scampi, plaice nor haddock dent the popularity of cod in the West Country. "Haddock is popular for fish and chips in Yorkshire," he said. "Rock salmon and skate in London and East Anglia. Down here, we're cod-eaters, by as much as 98 per cent. But don't ask me why."

Business was beginning to hot up as we spoke and, staying round to witness half-a-dozen customers, I heard them all ask for vinegar on their chips. Still, at £2.50 for a *Daily Express* wrapping-full, Fishy Moore served not only the best but the best-value fish and chips along the length of my stream.

Would his sons take over the shop? "No, I'm the last in line," replied Fishy, scooping into his chips. "They've got other plans for their futures."

Shurton Bars

In the shadow of Hinkley Point Nuclear Power Station, not a mile from the blue walls of Plant 'B', lies a desolate beach of sea grass and pebbles called Shurton Bars. It was here, or at least with here in mind, that in the autumn of 1795 Coleridge composed *Lines Written at Shurton Bars*. The poem is his response to a melancholy letter from his future wife, Sara, who awaits his return to Bristol. The poem is garnished with Romantic lyricism. A glow-worm moves with 'green radiance' through the grass, and the sky is a 'starry wilderness on high'. At another point, Coleridge senses that Sara's soul 'hovers round my head'.

More excitingly, *Shurton Bars* is shot through with the troubled images, stark and surreal, that would become the hallmark of his later, greater work. To get the full feel of the poem, I took the hilly coastal path one evening, skirted round the power station, and dropped down on to the beach.

The tide was out, but turning, and now the beach stretched westward, vast and flat and empty. The pebbles and stones, tumbled smooth by thousands of tides, once again had been left black and glistening by the retreated sea water. The air bore that quick, fresh-foul smell of seaweed and fish. Not a soul was in sight. Souls are rarely in sight on Shurton Bars, I'd learned at the bar of the *Shurton Inn*.

To the east was Highbridge, where the River Brue ends its journey. Offshore in the shipping lanes, where the Bristol Channel meets the Severn estuary, lie two small, unpopulated, islands: the suitably named Steep Holm, a craggy nature reserve and bird sanctuary, and, further out, the even more suitably named Flat Holm, with its lighthouse flashing three times every ten seconds. The lighthouse, now de-manned and 'solarised', casts a beam of fifteen nautical miles.

In 1736 sixty soldiers had been drowned when a vessel was wrecked near the Holms. The Society of Merchant Venturers in Bristol had already called for a lighthouse to protect their shipping; they controlled much of the trade from Africa and America to England. In response to their demands, a light was first shown on Flat Holm on 1st December 1737.

I could see the Nuclear Power Station off my shoulder – if I looked. But I chose not to look. Instead, I made myself as comfortable as possible against a boulder and, while the light held, read over the ninety-six lines of *Shurton Bars* on Shurton Bars.

It's harrowing stuff and, like the *Rime of the Ancient Mariner*, is literally and figuratively drenched in dream. The dusk was settling in. The tide moved quickly; after the Bay of Fundy, between New Brunswick and Nova Scotia, the tidal range in the Bristol Channel is the second greatest in the world. Why, Coleridge asks in his poem, does 'Fancy rouse within my breast/ Dim-visag'd shapes of Dread?'

> Even there – beneath that light-house tower –
> In the tumultuous evil hour
> Ere Peace with Sara came
> Time was, I should have thought it sweet
> To count the echoings of my feet,
> And watch the storm-vex'd flame.

The storm rages on, within and without.

> The tears that tremble down your cheek,
> Shall bathe my kisses chaste and meek
> In Pity's dew divine;
> And from your heart the sighs that steal
> Shall make your rising bosom feel
> The answering swell of mine!

> How oft, my Love! With shapings sweet
> I paint the moment, we shall meet!
> With eager speed I dart –
> I seize you in the vacant air,
> And fancy, with a husband's care
> I press you to my heart!

I could see a yacht, swinging at anchor, while a pair of yachtsmen busied themselves on its deck. Were they preparing to set out for the New World? If asked, would I sign on?

With mixed feelings, I realize that America, not England, has made me. On my journey down the stream, I'd learned much about England, good and ill, and reluctantly grown to ignore Charles Dickens' injunction: 'If the past makes such a bid for our attention, the present may escape us.'

I realize that I've been searching for a nostalgia I never knew: scavenging for parts of a warplane on Pennard Hill; the New Zealand boy killed in the plane crash; the chrome landing lights. My memories, filtered and ordered from childhood, are not of cunning cricket shots, nor of bulrushes flourishing in farm ponds like 'Lake Titicaca'. I'm a visitor here, an outsider. I'm stuck.

I think of the old Italian lady, still stumbling through English, who never was at home in England. But if I were to take that boat to America, I'd long to get back home to England. I'm here and, unavoidably, it's now. I can't, and don't, and won't, entertain the fantasy of getting aboard that boat to America. I'll remain a foreigner, an observer, a guest, an American, even when Ray Loxton digs me a hole, makes room for me in the crowded West Bradley churchyard.

Turning, I see Glastonbury Tor, back in the misty distance. West Bradley, off to the east and tucked out of sight, wouldn't be much farther along. I climb to my feet and start towards the River Brue and Bradley Brook. It may take me a while to get there.

At least I'll know the way.

Index of people